Human Motivation and the Dynamic Calculus

Human Motivation and the Dynamic Calculus

Raymond B. Cattell

PRAEGER

PRAEGER SPECIAL STUDIES • PRAEGER SCIENTIFIC

New York • Philadelphia • Eastbourne, UK
Toronto • Hong Kong • Tokyo • Sydney

Library of Congress Cataloging in Publication Data

Cattell, Raymond Bernard, 1905–
    Human motivation and the dynamic calculus.

    Bibliography: p.
    Includes index.
    1. Motivation (Psychology)—Mathematical
models.   I. Title.
BF503.C38   1984   153.8   84-15153
ISBN 0-03-072009-5

Published in 1985 by Praeger Publishers
CBS Educational and Professional Publishing
A Division of CBS, Inc.
521 Fifth Avenue, New York, New York 10175 U.S.A.

© 1985 by Praeger Publishers

56789   145   987654321

Printed in the United States of America on acid–free paper.

Contents

Preface

The dynamic calculus has now been in the public domain of psychology for nearly half a century (Cattell, 1935; 1940; 1943). Except for a small band of sophisticated, multivariate experimentalists, however, its incorporation into general psychological thinking has been slow. I have wondered whether this is entirely because of the general lack of training in multivariate methods or due partly also to the lack of a single clearly written exposition. In 1975 Dennis Child and I produced a direct account in *Motivation and Dynamic Structure* which, however, seems to have been regarded as too difficult for undergraduate classes as presently educated in science and mathematics. Consequently, I have decided to present the essence in the present more modest but concentrated form.

This is intended for the serious undergraduate student of psychology, who wants to get away from the innumerable and mostly superficial verbal discussions in order to find out what is experimentally established. I must admit I have never been able to reconcile myself to the aversion of the undergraduate psychologist to mathematical models—educators generally are at last awakening to the dearth of scientifically and mathematically trained students in this country.

In response to the realistic needs of the subject, what I present here is be no means complex. Undergraduates in classes in chemistry, physics, engineering, and biology readily face more complex calculations in their instruction. In any case, I have this time sought also to clarify the issues in verbal terms, and I launch this small book with the hope that it will become an indispensable part of the education in motivation of every psychologist.

Because of its condensation the book will generally need teaching as well as reading. It should be a guide to research especially for if the numerous promising tag ends exposed here for research are energetically followed up, such a transformation as will alter the practice of clinical, industrial, and educational psychology in less than a generation may be expected. The psychologist qualified in the next decade should be fully able to avail himself of the new methods.

Human Motivation and the Dynamic Calculus

1   The Nature of Motivation

Human motivation is the central theme common to all branches of psychology. Relatively few psychologists realize how much its study has been changed by the work of multivariate experimental psychologists. No longer can we take the verdicts of Freud, Jung, Adler, and their clinical followers of the seventies as what science has to say. Arcane statistical methods and ingeniously designed experiments have opened up a new domain of knowledge but it is not beyond the capacity of any qualified psychologist to enter this new domain and apply the emerging principles to his own field of endeavor.

Intensive study of the area's problems is available in *Motivation and Dynamic Structure*, Cattell and Child (1975) and in *Personality and Learning Theory*, Vol. 2, Cattell (1980), but I write the present text as a more digestible outline for the general student and a pointer to the research expeditions now possible for the graduate student and practitioner.

Since all sciences get their first laws from measurement, the foundation of a science of motivation begins with achieving measurement of motivation strengths. This is something that the clinician aspires to reach "by eye" and the animal experimenter by hours of deprivation of food and the like. The first human motivation measurement attempts began with the 1963 monograph, *The Nature and Measurement of Components of Motivation* and associated articles of Cattell, Maxwell, Light, & Unger (1949); Cattell, Heist, Heist, & Stewart (1950); Cattell, Radcliffe, & Sweney (1963); Cattell & Horn (1963); and Cattell & Baggaley (1956). From psychologists they gathered all the signs that had been found useful in detecting interest in a course of action about an object. It was their aim to take two or three diverse interests, measure each of them on thirty or more of these devices, and intercorrelate

1

people's scores to see which devices correlated most highly with the pool of all.

However, first one must define **interest in a course of action**. All action is undertaken in a field of stimulus situations. It has seemed appropriate, therefore, to define as a unit **attitude**, a course of action undertaken in a given situation. An attitude, therefore, has the parts indicated verbally thus:

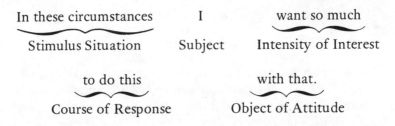

Any interest can be expressed in this form. It brings a new model of attitude away from the **for** or **against** abstraction of the polling booth into an emotional space where the course of response can express any combination of our emotional resources. As we shall see soon, the dynamic calculus permits the emotional roots of any attitude to be quantitatively discovered and set down.

For the moment we are concerned with finding out how the strength of interest in the course of action can be found for **any** attitude. The objective devices experimented upon included

1. psychoanalytic defenses (fantasy, true and naive projection, autism, and rationalization) as separated out by Cattell and Wenig (1952) factor analytically
2. physiological measures such as GSR (Galvanic Skin Reflex), blood pressure changes, etc.
3. laboratory measures of memory, perception, retroactive inhibition, decision time, etc.
4. new measures of distraction, perseveration, warm-up speed, and other signs alleged to be indicative of interest strength in men and animals.

When these devices were intercorrelated—over diverse attitudes—the same pattern of seven or eight distinct factors appeared. These have been named as follows:

1. **Alpha** or id component—loading such measures as autism, fantasy, distortion of reasoning, spoken preference, and projection

2. **Beta** or ego strength—loading information on the interest, free association speed, rate of learning a new language, perceptual integration, and quicker warm-up rate

3. **Gamma** or superego—loading superego projection, low perseveration, availability of associations, criterion utility, and some autism

4. **Delta** or physiological component—evading decision speed, GSR, blood pressure change, retroactive inhibition, hidden figures, and persistence

5. **Epsilon** or complex indicator—loading interference in reminiscence, GSR, threat response, cue memory, criterion utility, low persistence, and low reminiscence

6. **Zeta** or temperamental component—loading decision speed and strength, impulsiveness, low fluency, and low hidden figures

7. **Eta** or expectancy—loading high fluency on action cues, high action persistence, and high hidden figures.

Straightaway we have to recognize a psychometric fallacy in ascribing a single score to an individual on a particular attitude. Such a score—alas, commonly leaned upon in social psychology—is a composite of unknown composition.

The nature of these seven primary components is still, in part, a mystery. Without psychoanalytic inclinations one may nevertheless see the first three as corresponding to Freud's trio, but are they perhaps, alternatively, **ability** or **personality** traits? The content does not fit any known such traits nor do these factors correlate with fixed traits. Furthermore, for the same individual in different attitudes they correlate little. The final test of their uniqueness to motivation and their statelike quality is that they show up also in dR-technique, the factoring of difference scores compared to R-technique using absolute scores, and P-technique, i.e., when score **differences** from occasion to occasion are correlated, they still appear as factors.

However, all this later checking is on small numbers and few instances so that the mystery of their nature is still with us. Nevertheless, progress has been made by taking the correlations among these factors and factoring them to second order factors. Thereupon two major factors and a smaller third factor appear. The relations of the two major factors are shown in Figure 1-1.

On inspecting these components one feels an understanding at once. The ego and superego come together in what has become called the **Integrated** (I) factor and the **Unintegrated** (U) factor, which contains the id, the physiological and other unconscious primaries.

The U and the I measures are now mainly used in practical clinical work because they indicate different origins in an interest. Incidentally, without multivariate analysis the naive course would have been to take the **pool** of **all** device measures as the criterion of motivation strength, whereas Figure 1-1 shows the U and the I components are virtually **un**correlated entities denying this single score.

The present theory is that the I component represents that part of the interest which has been realized in life, showing itself in information in the area, rate of new learning, and availability of associations. The U component, on the other hand, is that part of an interest that has never come to terms with reality, showing itself in fantasy and physiology. The ordinary verbal preference statement of interest proves to have substantial U in it as well as some I.

The further clinical and experimental evidence now coming in shows that the U component alters more with stimulation and that it may gradually shift into the I component as psychotherapy proceeds. A high U score in an interest relative to I score is thus a sign that the individual has outer difficulties and inner conflicts in expressing that interest. Thus $(U - I)$ is a measure of maladjustment or conflict in the specific area of behavior being tested.

One theory of the roughly zero correlation of U and I is that (a) individuals differ in the strength of the pool of interest from which U and I arise, and this would lead to a high positive correlation, and (b) that I is what is not U. The latter would produce a strong negative correlation. The near-zero correlation found is the combined result of these two forces with the common size of source slightly predominating. This can be tested by P-technique where the common amount would not be expected to vary much from day to day, while U and I transformation would and the correlation should become negative.

The roles of U and I will be discussed again here under clinical applications, but for the present we must note that the total interest strength among individual factors falls into a U or I component and a

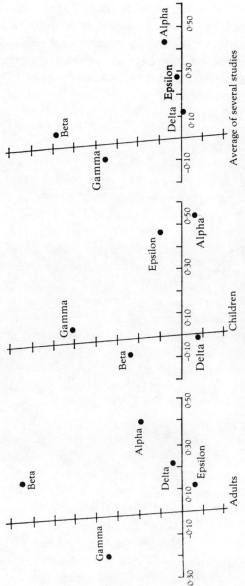

Relation of primaries to the secondary motivation components, U and I

FIGURE 1-1. Second order maturation components: *U* and *I*. Relation of primaries to the secondary motivation components, *U* and *I*.

third smaller factor which has been called persistence versus impulsiveness (Cattell et al., 1979).

Although the full nature of U and I remains to be understood, there is no doubt that they represent the bulk of what we can empirically call the strength of interest in an attitude—as shown by their correlations with time and money spent on an interest. In what follows we shall describe how many attitudes measured (each with its appropriate content of words, etc.) on these devices can tell us much about the dynamic structure of the average citizen.

2   The Human Dynamic
Structures—I: Ergs

The dynamic structure of an individual is probably more subject to change than the trait modalities we call ability and temperament traits. Nevertheless, it should be possible to reveal it by the same correlational, factor analytic methods that have clarified the structures in trait modalities.

Accordingly, a deliberately very broad array of attitudes to cover the totality of common interests was measured by the objective test (nonquestionnaire) devices which have been polished above and the attitudes intercorrelated. If, for example, strong interest in one's work goes with reduced interest in the family, a negative correlation would be expected; and if being a Republican goes with stronger interest in saving money, a positive correlation would be expected.

The list of attitudes tried out can be seen along with the factor matrices for the motivation devices in Cattell and Child (1975). Here we shall deal only with the outcome, which was a series of factors that proved to be of two kinds. About half of them appeared to be instincts (**ergs** as we finally call them) in which numerous attitudes were brought together, all sharing subsidiation to the same drive goal and having the same emotional quality. In Table 2–1 (see following page) they are exemplified in two factor loading patterns.

It will be seen that the highest loaded attitude measures are those nearest to the most direct expression, respectively, of the need to escape danger and sexual expressions. Further down on each list are expansions one might think of at first such as a desire for reduction of income tax (capacity to save), in fear and interest in music (in the case of sex). Such findings, however, do support clinical observation of roundabout satis-

TABLE 2-1. Attitude Loadings Defining Two Ergs

Security-seeking (fear, escape)

	Loadings
I want my country to get more protection against the terror of the atom bomb	.5
I want to see any formidable militaristic power that actively threatens us attacked and destroyed	.5
I want to see the danger of death by accident and disease reduced	.4
I want to see those responsible for inflation punished	.4
I want never to be an insane patient in a mental hospital	.4
I want to see a reduction of income tax for those in my bracket	.3
I want to take out more insurance against illness	.3
I want to become proficient in my career	.3
I want my country to have power and influence in the world	.3
I like to take part in political arguments	.3

Attitudes defining the sex erg

	Loadings
I want to fall in love with a beautiful woman	.5
I want to satisfy my sexual needs	.5
I like sexual attractiveness in a woman	.5
I like to see a good movie now and then	.4
I like a novel with love interest and a ravishing heroine	.4
I like to enjoy smoking and drinking	.4
I want to see more good restaurants serving attractive food	.3
I want to listen to music	.3
I want to travel and explore the world	.3

factions and sublimations. Similar patterns are found (see Cattell & Child, 1975, p. 29) for further drives like gregariousness, parental, protective, pitying behavior, exploration (curiosity), self-assertion, etc. up to a total as shown in Table 2–2.

There are doubtless others still to be found by multivariate experiment, especially among more subtle and fragmentary tendencies such as Jung envisaged. The same patterns are found in children (Cattell & Child, 1975, p. 35) and in adult (Cattell & Cross, 1952) by P-technique.

It is interesting to notice that these drive patterns are approached

TABLE 2-2. List of Discovered Human Ergs

Goal title	Emotion	Status of evidence
Food-seeking	Hunger	Replicated factor; measurement battery exists
Mating	Sex	Replicated factor; measurement battery exists
Gregariousness	Loneliness	Replicated factor; measurement battery exists
Parental	Pity	Replicated factor; measurement battery exists
Exploration	Curiosity	Replicated factor; measurement battery exists
Escape to security	Fear	Replicated factor; measurement battery exists
Self-assertion	Pride	Replicated factor; measurement battery exists
Narcistic sex	Sensuousness	Replicated factor; measurement battery exists
Pugnacity	Anger	Replicated factor; measurement battery exists
Acquisitiveness	Greed	Replicated factor; measurement battery exists
Appeal	Despair	Factor, but of uncertain independence
Rest-seeking	Sleepiness	Factor, but of uncertain independence
Constructiveness	Creativity	Factor, but of uncertain independence
Self-abasement	Humility	Factor, but of uncertain independence
Disgust	Disgust	Factor absent for lack of markers
Laughter	Amusement	Factor absent for lack of markers

more closely in the literature by the lists of Darwin, McDougall, Lorenz, and others dealing with primates than by the relatively arbitrary conceptions of Freud (1915), Murray (1936) and Maslow (1935), which are still set out in students' textbooks as the lists of innate drives. The term **erg** has been introduced for these drives on an experimental foundation, using the same term as in physics from the Greek for work or **energy**; since these drives are the ultimate roots of human effort and activity. In each of them we see:

1. a biologically prescribed goal to which each of the loaded attitudes ultimately leads
2. an emotion specific to the given erg
3. an innate tendency to pay attention to stimuli of a particular cue nature in regard to the goal
4. an innate foundation for the drive, physiologically indicatable.

The last has not been directly demonstrated so far by the usual behavior genetic methods (twin and MAVA (Multiple Abstract Variance Analysis)). It will not prove easy to do so without averaging many occasion measures on each subject because it is in the nature of ergic tension to be very situation-dependent. (Note **ergic** rhymes with **allergic**). However, the striking similarity of these factor analytically discovered patterns to those seen by ethologists like Lorenz (1967) in primates, mammals, and birds justifies the contingent assumption that they **are** innate predispositions to attend, to feel, and to act toward a given goal.

3   The Human Dynamic Structures —II: Sems

Alongside the ergic factors appeared a second series of factors which have been called sentiments, or *sems* for short. In each of these, as illustrated in Table 3–1, some institution—home, school, sport, career, country—was obviously the object of a collection of attitudes.

These factors also appeared in P-technique, longitudinal analysis in the single individual though with apparently somewhat smaller day-to-day variance than with ergs (Cattell & Cross, 1952). They seem to represent sets of attitudes that people **learn** to acquire around objects important to them. If we know what objects stand for a person's **sentiments**, we know a good deal about how that person will react in life. We explain these attitudes making up a factor by the fact that all have been learned by repeated exposure to much the same level. Thus, if we have a population of people in which some have exposed themselves to church a good deal and others a little, we should expect correlations to appear among such attitudes as "I want to see organized religion maintained" and "I want to feel that I am in touch with God." These clusters will thus appear as factors (sems) with a certain object central to each.

Table 3–2 presents a list of sentiments that have been found in our culture by various approaches. In this case we have included results from nonobjective, verbal statement tests such as those of Guilford et al. (1954) and Strong (1949), since we would suppose that the integrated I component would be strong here as in complexes except in objects that are unconscious. Incidentally, the objective device (U and I) battery should pick up unconscious as well as conscious structures, since it registers connections of interest whether conscious or unconscious, particularly through primary motivation component epsilon, ϵ. This we

11

TABLE 3-1. Attitudes Found Loading Three Sems

Religious sentiment

	Loadings
I want to feel that I am in touch with God, or some principle in the universe that gives meaning and help in my struggles	.6
I want to see the standards of organized religion maintained or increased throughout our lives	.6
I want to have my parents' advice and to heed their wishes in planning my affairs	.4
I want my parents never to be lacking the necessities of comfortable living	.3
I do not want to see birth control available at all	.2
I want more protection against the atom bomb	.2
I want my country to be the most powerful and influential	.2
I want to help the distressed, wherever they are	.2
I do not want to spend more time playing cards	.2

Sentiment to profession (Air Force)*

	Loadings
I want to make my career in the Air Force	.70
I like the excitement and adventure of combat flying	.63
I want to get technical education such as the Air Force provides	.58
I enjoy commanding men and taking the responsibilities of a military leader	.44
I do not want to take more time to enjoy rest and to sleep later in the mornings	.41
I like being up in an airplane	.41
I want to satisfy my sense of duty to my country by enlisting in its most important defense arm in threatening times	.39
I want to become first-rate at my Air Force job	.36
I do not want to spend more time at home puttering around	.36

Sports and games

	Loadings
I like to watch and talk about athletic events	.75
I like to take an active part in sports and athletics	.63
I enjoy hunting and fishing trips	.27
I do not like to make things with my hands in wood, metal, or clay, to paint, etc.	.20
I like to get into a fight, particularly if my rights are involved	.20
I like to spend (some of) my spare time playing cards with the fellows	.16

TABLE 3-2. List of Discovered Human Sems

S^1 *Profession* (1)
S^2 *Parental family* (1)
S^3 *Wife, sweetheart* (1)
S^4 *The self-sentiment* (1). Physical and psychological self
S^5 *Superego* (1)
S^6 *Religion*. This has emphasis on doctrine and practice, on high social and low esthetic values (1) (4) (7) (8)
S^7 *Sports and fitness*. games, physical activity, hunting, military activity (1) (2) (3)
S^8 *Mechanical interests* (1) (2) (5)
S^9 *Scientific interests*. High theoretical, low political; math. (2) (3) (4) (5) (6) (7) (9)
S^{10} *Business-economic*. Money administrative (2) (3) (4) (5)
S^{11} *Clerical interests* (2) (4)
S^{12} *Esthetic expressions* (2) (10)
S^{13} *Esthetic-literary appreciation*. Drama
S^{14} *Outdoor-manual*. Rural, nature-loving, gardening, averse to business and "cerebration" (2) (5) (6)
S^{15} *Theoretical-logical*. Thinking, precision (2) (8) (10)
S^{16} *Philosophical-historical*. Language, civics, social-cultural, esthetic rather than economic (2) (3) (6) (7)
S^{17} *Patriotic-political* (1) (7)
S^{18} *Sedentary-social games*. Diversion, play club and pub sociability; cards (2) (10)
S^{19} *travel-geography*. Possibly Guilford's autism here
S^{20} *Education-school attachment*
S^{21} *Physical-home-decoration-furnishing*
S^{22} *Household-cooking*
S^{23} *News-communication*. Newspaper, radio, TV
S^{24} Clothes, self-adornment
S^{25} Animal pets
S^{26} Alcohol
S^{27} Hobbies not already specified

*References:
(1) Cattell *et al.* (4 studies)
(2) Guildford *et al.* (1954)
(3) Thurstone (1931)
(4) Gundlach and Gerum (1931)
(5) Torr (1953)
(6) Carter, Pyles, Bretnall (1935)
(7) Ferguson, Humphreys, Strong (1941)
(8) Lurie (1937)
(9) Strong (1949)
(10) Thorndike (1935)
See also
(11) Cottle (1950)
(12) Hammond (1945)
(13) Crissy and Daniel (1939)
(14) Vernon (1949)
(15) Miller (1968)

believe to be complex-indicating because the combination of high GSR with poor memory for stimulating cues was found by Ikin, Pear, & Thouless (1924) to be characteristic of complexes. However, because complexes depend on **individual** experience, we would not expect to find—and have not found—examples in R-technique but only in P-technique studies (Cattell & Cross, 1952; Birkett & Cattell, 1978).

Any psychologist familiar with the past 50 years of writing in this field will recognize that ergs went out of fashion in the late twenties and came back only gradually as evidence of their basic importance accumulated. Meanwhile, Allport (1938), for one, met the needs of the sociologist rebels against the innate by positing **functional autonomy**, the notion that a habit pursued long enough loses its attachment to the drive goal and becomes a motive in itself. Freud remained adamant and was completely opposed to this. His clinical experience taught him that all behavior ultimately **subsidiated** (to use Murray's useful term) to innate goals. Our position is that **subgoals** on the way to the final ergic goal achieve a motivating capacity by learning, which sometimes seems to support Allport. However, all sems ultimately are motivated by ergic goals to which the behavior in them subsidiates. For example, "I want to be in touch with God" subsidiates to the goal of the appeal erg among other ergic goals, and "I enjoy commanding men...." subsidiates to the goal of the self-assertive erg.

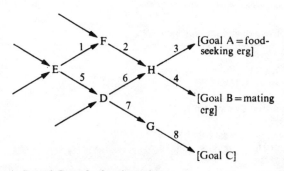

A, B, and C are final ergic goals;
D, E, F, G, and H are sub-goal stimuli;
1 to 8 are attitudes forming the subsidiation chain.
Thus, attitude 1 could be "I want to qualify as an interpreter"
        attitude 2 could be "I want to earn a living"
        attitude 3 could be "I want to eat"
        attitude 4 could be "I want to get married"

FIGURE 3-1. Sems as subgoals in the dynamic lattice.

TABLE 3-3. Super Ego and Self-sem (With Other Sems in Adults and Children)

Sems	Major Attitudes	Average loadings	
		Adult	Children
Self-sentiment	To control impulses and mental processes	40	32
	Never to damage self-respect	35	27
	To excel in my line of work	38	
	To maintain good reputation	37	34
	Never to become insane	39	
	to be responsible, in charge of things	31	
	To know about science, art, literature	31	
	To know more about myself	33	
	To grow up normally		28
Superego sentiment	To satisfy sense of duty to church, parents, etc.	41	
	Never to be selfish in my acts	41	
	To avoid sinful expression of sex needs	33	
	To avoid drinking, gambling—i.e., "vice"	21	
	To maintain good self-control	28	31
	To admire and respect father		28
Religious sentiment	To worship God		34
	To go to church		33
Career sentiment	To learn skills required for job	34	
	To continue with present career plans	33	
	To increase salary and status	27	
Sweetheart sentiment	To bring gifts to sweetheart	51	
	To spend time with sweetheart	41	

Thus, the dynamic structure factor which we find as a sem factor is really an intermediate goal on the way to satisfaction of several distinct ergs. In subsidiation terms it appears in the dynamic lattice as shown in Figure 3–1.

It will be seen that distinguishing ergic from semic patterns is not difficult by inspection alone. For the former, load attitudes different in their social setting (see "insanity" and "insurance" in Table 2–1) but common in purpose ("security" in this case), whereas sems, conversely, bring together attitudes common in their social object but differing in their ergic goal ("assertiveness" and "duty" in Table 3–1).

In this connection, in the period of ergic unpopularity the term **secondary drive** was brought into use by animal experimenters essentially for an acquired interest which we now call a sem. The use of **drive** is misleading for the new interest is anything but a single drive. It is a **collection** of drives reinforced around a single object.

Two sems that deserve special mention are those named the **self-sentiment** and the **superego**. These stand out clearly in Table 3–3.

The first constitutes the set of attitudes that grow up around the self concept, which is an ideational object just like any other sentiment. However, as Table 3–3 shows, it is more poorly put together in children than in adults. Incidentally, as Sweney and Cattell's work (1961) shows, **most** sentiment structure is more fragmentary and unintegrated in children. His results (1961) show it to a degree which is rather surprising, though one realizes how transient the formation of sems is in that period.

Obviously, sem structure will differ as to number and nature in different countries whereas ergs should be much the same; that is to say, they should be the same in number and nature but different in the attitudes with lower loadings. For example, in an Italian population, we found self-assertion loading desire to take a position in a hierarchy; whereas this was relatively low in the United States, while desire to run one's own business in freedom was higher in the United States.

Since a person's score on an ergic tension or the level of development of a sem is a weighted sem of the objective test scores on the attitude involved, we must expect some problems in comparing scores across cultures, but no more than the usual psychometric rules apply to comparisons within cultures (Cattell, 1969; 1970).

4   The Dynamic Lattice and Its Tracing

If we ask a male why he pursues a given attitude course of action, he will usually name a more or less immediate subgoal. For example, to "Why do you do exercises every morning?" he may reply, "To get fit enough to join the rowing club." If we next ask, "Why join the rowing club?," he will name more remote goals such as "That I may please my girl friend, Jane." The first of these attitudes, we have agreed, is best described as **subsidiated** to the second.

If we continue the psychological exploration of motives, a whole subsidiation chain will generally be found. An example is attitude 17 in Figure 4–1, through a series of subgoals ultimately leading to an ergic goal beyond the last question, which might be, "Why do you want to eat?" There is no real answer: the ergic goal is sufficient in itself.

If we pursued this inquiry widely enough like a psychologist with a patient, we will find that we are not dealing with a single chain but with many chains which crisscross at subgoals as shown in Figure 4–1. A subgoal, e.g., a sem, such as "keeping my bank account positive" is fed by several courses of action and in turn subsidiates to several further courses of action which ultimately lead to ergic goals.

As Freud found, simply asking people why they do this or that is not adequate. The person may not really know the reason behind an action—the root is unconscious—or may be unwilling to tell. By alternative experimental means there are two main possibilities: (1) **path obstruction** or (2) **factor analysis**. The latter, which we have shown to work in Chapters 2 and 3, takes measures across a set of attitudes, e.g., those cut by the line X - Y in Figure 4–1, intercorrelates them across a set of people or a set of occasions in P-technique and finds their factor structure. The answer will be in the form of ergic and semic factor tables

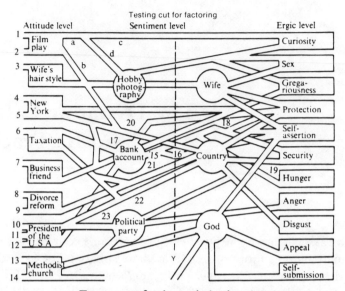

Fragment of a dynamic lattice showing attitude
subsidiåtion, sentiment structure, and ergic goals
Source: Cattell (1965).

FIGURE 4-1. Illustration of the dynamic lattice. Source: Cattel (1965).

and their loadings on the given attitudes. From the given factor tables
which show to which ergs and sentiments attitudes contribute, analysis
will permit us to restore the dynamic lattice, with some care and
ingenuity.

The path obstruction method is quite different. It requires that we
block one of the subject's attitude courses and then measure what
happens to the strength of others. The principle is set out in Figure 4-1
(above) and involves what is sometimes called stimulus equivalences or
substitution of symptoms. If we prevent the individual from utilizing
path d in Figure 4-1, then the need to satisfy curiosity and sex ergs will
cause some growth in the traffic of path c, and in b, etc. The proof that
both d and b subsidiate to subgoal hobby is therefore evidenced by
changes in the strength of paths a, b, c, d, and some others. This may be
said to involve the **hydraulic principle** because it is analogous to what
happens when we try to find how pipes are connected by observing
changes of flow at various faucets. Up to a point the same calculations
will fit both instances. In practice we need not forbid the subject some

path entirely, but we can reduce interest in it by giving information that it is too costly or impracticable, while observing the other interests. For example, if Johnny goes to the swimming pool when he is told that his football has gone flat, we may assume that there are equivalent paths to some common goal, an athletic sem.

Although discovering the dynamic lattice of a patient is often the primary condition of clinical diagnosis and treatment, it is unfortunately true that neither of the above methods is usually applied. Some simpler method, like free association, hypnotism, or whatever is commonly clinically used, gives a rough solution, which unfortunately does not lead to a quantitative answer.

However, in a few fully reported cases P-technique factoring has been used, which shall be briefly described here and then more fully later. In this technique, some 20 to 40 attitudes are measured each day for about 100 occasions on one person (hence "P"). It is assumed that the opportunities of daily life and the impacts of the consulting room will disturb the level of ergs and sems and show what their connection to ergs by the changing strength of attitudes and sems is. A factor analysis reveals these connections and also permits the daily strength of ergic tensions to be measured and plotted. Figure 4-2 shows the plot for a young man studied by Cattell and Cross (1952). In this case a daily diary clearly shows that the ergs and sems are responsive to the kinds of situational stimuli that we would expect. For example, his self-assertion is stimulated by being accepted for an important part in a play, and his narcism rises markedly as he appears before the footlights.

Another example is that of a clergyman who became an alcoholic (Birkett & Cattell, 1978). He was examined for 100 days on the MAT (U and I measures separate) and/or a measure of the symptom strength. (The MAT, Motivation Analysis Test, is a standardized objective motivation test described later.) Factored together these revealed the connections shown in Table 4-1, which are also expressed in a path coefficient diagram in the original (Birkett & Cattell, 1978).

It becomes evident that the symptom correlations are very similar for U and I, and that the need for alcohol is highest when the sentiment to the wife, the self-sentiment, and the narcsistic needs are low, and the fear, pugnacity, superego, and sex ergs are high. Similar studies showing the power of P-technique to unravel the dynamic lattice are found in Kline and Grindley (1974), Cattell and Luborsky (1950) and Shotwell, Hurley and Cattell (1961). The arduousness and complexity have

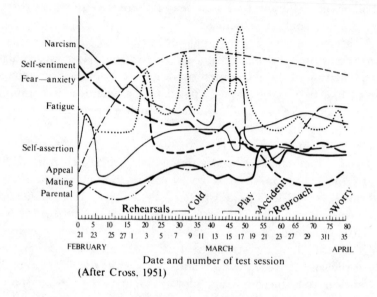

(After Cross, 1951)

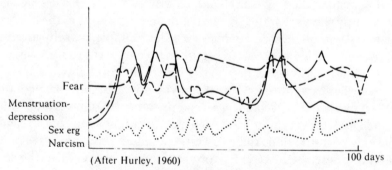

(After Hurley, 1960)   100 days

Ergic tension (and sentiment) response to stimulus (S),
internal state (P), and goal satisfaction (G)

FIGURE 4-2. Ergs and sems in two P-technique experiments. Ergic
tension (and sentiment) response to stimulus (S), internal state (P), and
goal satisfaction (G).

20

TABLE 4-1. Alcoholism Symptom Correlations Diagnosed by P-technique

Component of Alcohol Score	U		I		Total
Component of Predictor Score	I	U	I	U	Total
Fear	25	30	25	27	29
Assertion	-11	00	-09	-01	-05
Pugnacity	15	12	18	12	15
Super Ego	18	19	23	25	23
Wife Sentiment	-44	-45	-37	-45	-46
Sex Erg	29	29	26	25	29
Narcistic Erg	-54	-64	-48	-60	-61
Self Sentiment	-24	-20	-22	-22	-23
Career Sentiment	02	-01	00	03	07
Home Sentiment	-02	14	03	05	07
Appeal Erg	-01	-14	06	-10	03

The consistency across U & I measures is remarkably high. Only in Super Ego is there a suggestion of difference.

nevertheless kept this very positive method of analysis from wider use, though Cattell and Birkett (1980) have recently shown it will work with fewer occasions and the help of a movie film.

It will be recognized that in tracing the loading of a symptom to dynamic structure factors we are essentially saying what causes it. The results in Table 4–1 can be written in an equation which in the higher loadings would be:

$$A_{ik} = 0.29E_{f\ ik} + 0.23S_{ss\ ik} - 0.46S_{w\ ik} + 0.29E_{s\ ik}$$
$$- 0.61E_{n\ ik} - 0.23S_{se\ ik} \qquad (4\text{-}1)$$

where the E's are **ergic tensions** on f = fear, s = sex, and n = narcsism, and the S's are **sems** as in ss = self sem, w = wife, and se = superego. A negative sign means that the dynamic trait contributes negatively, i.e., the symptom is high when the trait becomes low. By inserting the individual i scores on the dynamic traits on the day, k, from this we can predict what the need for alcohol will be. This insight is the necessary diagnostic preliminary to psychotherapy.

5   Some Principles in the Interrelations of Dynamic Traits

It behooves us next to clarify the above findings of ergs and sems in terms of what can be done with them in the dynamic calculus. We last looked at the *use* of the dynamic behavioral equation. In its most general form this aid to prediction and estimation is as follows:

$$a_{hijk} = b_{hjkei}E_{1i} + \ldots + b_{hjken}E_{ni} + b_{hjkmi}M_{1i}$$

$$\ldots + b_{hjkmo}M_{0i} \qquad (5\text{-}1)$$

This possibly fearsome-looking equation has footnotes: h = stimulus, i = individual, j = particular attitude, and k = situation. It will be noted that stimulus, h, and situation, k, are kept distinct, since the same stimulus, e.g., a friend, can be encountered in many different situations, k's. Thus, a_{hijk} describes the magnitude of an interest, a, of type, j, in response to a stimulus, h, in situation, k. The b's are behavioral indices—literally factor loadings. They are peculiar both to the stimulus response situation, hjk, and to the particular dynamic trait, E_1, through E_n and M_1 through M_0 in sems, i.e., there are n ergs and o sems included in the prediction which is just equation (4-1) put in general terms.

It will be recognized that the b values mathematically form a vector. If there were only two of them, we could represent a_{hjk} by a line of given length and direction (Figure 5-1). Being a vector, it can be added and subtracted from other vectors as shown in Figure 5-2. Knowing how we can add and subtract vectors in this simple visual way, the reader will appreciate that we can find a couple of attitudes that will sum to the

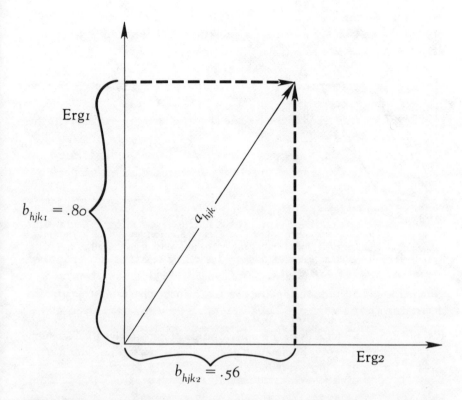

FIGURE 5-1. Representation of an attitude as a vector quanity. An attitude a_{hij} represented as a vector loaded b_{hjk_1} on Erg1 and b_{hjk_2} on Erg2. Permission to come

same satisfaction as some given attitude that has to be abandoned for some reason.

The behavioral equation (5–1) above is usually obtained by factor analyzing measures of behavior, a_{hijk}, with other behaviors and then is sometimes called a specification equation taken as a row from the factor pattern matrix. However, if we have good measures of the ergs and sems, we can instead simply correlate their scores with the a_{hijk} scores (and correct to weights as in partial equations, knowing the correlations among the ergs and sems). In Equation (5–1) we have not introduced a specific factor peculiar to a_{hjk}, supposing all of the interest strength being due to the common ergs and sems; but in practice there would usually be some variance in a_{hjk} unaccounted for, requiring a specific factor.

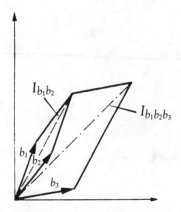

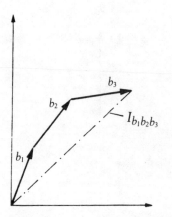

Method 1

$I_{b_1 b_2 b_3}$ is the final resultant found by first obtaining the resultant $I_{b_1 b_2}$ for b_1 and b_2 and then locating the resultant between $I_{b_1 b_2}$ and the remaining vector b_2 to give $I_{b_1 b_2 b_3}$.

Method 2

Join the vectors head to tail as shown. The line which joins the tail of b_1 to the head of b_3 is the same resultant $I_{b_1 b_2 b_3}$ as in Method 1.

Summation of attitude vectors for one sentiment to give total strength of interest $I_{b_1 b_2 b_3}$

FIGURE 5-2. Methods of summing attitude vectors to give total strength and character of interest. Summation of attitude vectors for one sentiment to give total strength of interest $Ib_1 b_2 b_3$.

If we have the scores of the person from the MAT tests, for example, on the ergs, E_1, E_2, etc, and the sems, M_1, M_2, etc., we can then estimate interest on the course of action a_{hijk} by multiplying each such score by the weight of the corresponding behavioral index, b, and adding the ten or more products. This is only an estimate, not an exact and true value for the subject because the b's are those common to all members of the population, not specific to the person Smith. If we want behavioral indices that are right for Smith, we have to do a P-technique factor experiment on Smith alone, and we shall then get weights not only for a given behavior but for a given behavior on a given occasion, b_{hjk} (k being the behavioral situation).

Let us repeat that h and k are different parts of the total situation in which the response, j, is made, h being the **focal stimulus**, to which Smith is attending and k the **ambient situation**, in which the reponse is made. Much behavioristic formulation omits this distinction and talks only of the stimulus; but if Smith is responding to an intelligence test item, h, in a quiet room or in a hot, noisy room, the latter **ambient** (surrounding) situation, k, will make quite a difference to the response and the equation for predicting it. **The total stimulus situation is** $(h + k)$.

It will be recognized that the vector of weights which we have described is peculiar to the given situation-response and thus can be used as a mathematical description of that situation. Later we shall see that it can be broken down by splitting b into two parts; but for the present let us recognize that these vectors challenge and belie the one-time assertion that "personality theorists neglect the situation." In fact, they are more precise about personality responses being predictable from situations than reflexologists are, counterwise, about bringing the vector of traits (E_I to E_4, M_I to M_o) into prediction of a conditioned response. Indeed, as we shall see later, these **vectors** (profiles) of situations can be used to find out exactly how much one situation psychologically resembles another—by putting them side by side. Thus, we have an objective basis for finding how many situation **types** there are and what they mean psychologically.

While we are dealing with the behavioral equation we should note that in Equation (5-1) we represent only the **dynamic** equation, and that in any actual behavior the other two modalities, abilities and temperament traits, would enter in thus:

$$a_{hijk} = \sum^{x=p} b_{hjkx} A_{xi} + \sum^{y=q} b_{hjky} P_{yi} + \sum^{z=r} b_{hjkzi} D_{zi} \qquad (5\text{-}2)$$

Here we use the summation sign, Σ, to indicate that we sum all p ability traits, A (with their appropriate weights), all q general personality factors, P, and all dynamic trait effects, D. This is an expression of the general recognition that all traits enter into all behavior. However, hitherto, in Equation (5-1) we have supposed that by a_{hijk} we are measuring only the dynamic **strength of interest** in the given response, and we should then use only the MAT, SMAT, School Motivation Analysis Test, or similar objective motivation component test in measuring a_{hijk}. In doing this we are reminded that there are U and I components or indeed all seven primaries in the total dynamic measure, so we could make separate a_{hijk} measures in the U and the I. Some clinicians are inclined to argue that ergs contribute largely to the U and sems largely to the I components. The basis for this argument is that U measures more unconscious and physiological primaries (see Figure 1-1, p.5) and I more of what is learned so that the sems, being learned, should show up with greater variance in I measures. This remains to be checked but has the support indicated. Obviously, measures of sems will not yield **only** I measures because they are supported by the ergs that achieve expression through them, but they may well prove richer in *I* measures than are the ergs.

We would suppose also that sem measures will have greater stability coefficients from occasion to occasion than ergic tension measures, which might vary with specific ergic stimuli and internal hormonal and appetitive conditions. As Table 5–1 shows, present evidence gives no support for such a difference, though all measures are lower than for measures of equal length on general personality factors.

This brings us to the relation of dynamic structures to personality and ability factors. The supposition is that, based on different types of actual performance, they will stand uncorrelated in different factor space. The evidence supports this except for those dynamic structure factors—self-sentiment, superego, and ego—that are of such a general nature that they also appear as factors in questionnaire and objective tests of personality. The extent of correlation is shown in Table 5–2.

Table 5–1. Stability Coefficients for Measure Dynamic Traits, Ergs and Sems

		Stability coefficients		
		Over five weeks*	Over six months†	
		Adults	Children	
Dynamic factor	Erg_iE & Sem_iS		I	U
Fear	E	.48	.29	.14
Mating	E	.51	.58	.20
Assertiveness	E	.53	.34	.23
Narcism	E	.53	.43	.17
Pugnacity	E	.41	.45	.20
Career	S	.39	—	—
Sweetheart	S	.47	—	—
Home–parental	S	.65	.23	.25
Superego	S	.46	.38	.07*
Self-sentiment	S	.69	.46	.05*
School sentiment	S	—	.39	.10*

Motivation Analysis Test Handbook (1964).

†Bartsch (1973, personal communication). Note the insignificant values (asterisks) in the U component of some sentiment factor amongst children.

E is an erg, S a sentiment.

TABLE 5-2. Relation of Dynamic Structures to General Personality Traits

Relation of dynamic modality factors to general personality factors

Dynamic Traits	A Affectia	B Intelligence	C Ego weakness	E Dominance	F Surgency	G Superego strength	H Parmia	I Premsia	L Protension	M Autia	N Shrewdness	O Guilt-proneness	Q_1 Radicalism	Q_2 Self-sufficiency	Q_3 Self-sentiment	Q_4 Ergic tension
Sex	.02	.15	.02	-.02	.11	-.30	-.11	-.06	.20	.31	.11	.27	.27	.19	-.31	-.31
Gregariousness	.33	.05	.15	-.01	.22	-.18	.17	-.06	-.08	.01	.01	.01	-.11	-.33	-.12	.03
Parental protectiveness	.06	-.15	.09	-.25	-.09	.12	-.08	.04	-.07	.01	-.15	.06	-.09	-.16	.03	.05
Exploration (curiosity)	-.14	.09	.01	.02	-.10	.07	-.06	.21	.01	.13	.09	.04	.29	.13	.09	-.00
Fear; escape	-.07	-.12	-.09	-.01	-.16	.19	.15	.01	-.06	-.17	-.02	-.20	.09	-.13	.27	-.23
Self-assertion	.24	.11	.06	.15	-.00	-.01	.32	-.06	-.20	.03	.03	-.06	.21	-.12	.07	-.10
Narcistic vs. superego	.02	.08	.05	.07	.13	-.37	-.12	-.15	.21	.35	.12	.22	.27	.22	-.39	.26
Air Force	.01	.01	.11	.23	.13	.14	.38	-.09	-.24	-.13	.13	-.38	-.05	-.07	.21	.41
Sports	-.00	-.11	.02	-.02	-.08	-.06	-.02	-.16	-.12	-.03	-.01	-.09	-.20	-.04	-.08	-.00
Religious sentiment	.01	-.18	.03	-.19	-.05	.26	.01	.20	-.14	-.22	-.16	-.12	-.34	-.33	.25	-.10
Mechanical materialistic interest	-.03	.10	.01	.10	.01	.11	.10	-.13	-.05	-.01	.04	-.12	.16	.15	.06	-.18
Self-sentiment	.11	.10	.04	.20	-.05	.13	.34	.05	-.31	-.15	-.02	-.22	.06	-.18	.34	-.25
Rest-seeking	-.10	.03	-.03	-.09	-.20	.10	-.04	-.04	-.02	.04	.06	.14	.10	.05	.05	.09

*Significant 1% level.

27

Here we notice, as significant but at a rather low level, the correlations of the self-sentiment (0.34) and the superego (0.37) with the corresponding 16 PF (Personality Factors) measures, and also an r of 0.38 of parmia to career, of 0.35 of autia with superego, of 0.22 of superego and guilt proneness, of –0.34 of radicalism and religious sentiment, of –0.33 of gregariousness and self-sufficiency (Q_2), of 0.39 of superego with self-sentiment, and of –0.41 of career with ergic tension (Q_4). We can readily see causes for most of these, and, of course, with correction for attenuation we might expect higher correlations between the two ways of measuring the self-sentiment and the superego, which have essentially the **same** trait meaning in the two scales.

A question often raised is whether gregarious need strength (in the MAT) and extroversion (on A, F, H, and Q_2) and self-assertiveness and dominance (E) should not be related. Table 5–2 shows appreciable relation in the former but relatively trivial relation in the latter. Clearly, we have to distinguish conceptually between a personality trait and a dynamic trait. An exviant person (extrovert in popular language) will have a greater gregarious interest; but this is a secondary derivative of his exviant personality, which suits him better to social interaction. In the case of dominance we see a self-assurance which may or may not be tied to a strong desire to assert oneself. (If Adler is right, the least secure might be most in need of assertion). In fact, in Table 5–2, we see assertiveness tied most to affectia and parmia. The personality traits and the dynamic traits do have a number of significant connections, but except for the self-sentiment and the superego sentiment they indicate a moderate and complex interdependence rather than any one-to-one alignment.

6   The Manner of Growth of Dynamic Traits and Unitary Factors

Ergic tension has been conceptually related to drive strength and need strength as shown in Equation 6-1.

$$E_{xk} = (S_k + Z)\,[x(C + H + I) + \{(P_k - aG_k) + (N_k - bG_s)\}]$$

$$\underbrace{}_{\text{Drive Strength}} \quad \underbrace{}_{\text{Appetite State Strength}}$$

$$\underbrace{\phantom{\text{Drive Strength Appetite State Strength}}}_{\text{Need Strength}}$$

$$\underbrace{\phantom{\text{Ergic Tension Strength全部}}}_{\text{Ergic Tension Strength}} \tag{6-1}$$

This conceives the measured ergic tension by the objective devices at E_{xk} as the result of multiplying the **need** strength, E_x, by the strength of the stimulus, $(s_k + Z)$. The Z in the latter is a constant to explain the fact that for some ergs ergic tension does not seem to disappear when all external provocation, s_k, becomes zero.

The need strength, drive strength at the time, regardless of provocation, is conceived of as having two parts, one permanent and one due to internal appetitive state at the time. The permanent part (drive strength) is determined by C, a constitutional, genetic component, H, an early history covering the Freudian concept of arrests in development through trauma, and I pecularities due to investment of the drive in the particular attitudes by which we choose to measure it. The appetitive state has two parts, one reduced by physiological gratification, G_p, and one by psychological gratification, G_p. The recency and magnitude of these will operate separately as rat experiments show. The appetitive part, especially $(P_k - aG_k)$, distinguishes the class of viscerogenic from aviscerogenic drives, which have no obvious visceral component (self-assertion, gregariousness, etc.). The a, x, b, and z are constants to give due weight to observed differences.

In an erg that we actually measure the ergic tension level is thus a complex derivative of underlying values which we can only infer from comparative experiment, but the unitary character as a factor arises from the unitary nature of the original drive. Of special interest in determining the rise of ergic tension is the modulator index, s_k, which we shall meet again later under **the modulation theory of states**.

The rise and development of sems presents a more complex problem. We have to account for a whole set of attitudes being learned to much the same level in any one person and different levels in different people if we are to account for sems as R-technique factors. Three processes have been theorized to account for this and also for the appearance of dR- and R-technique semic factors as follows:

1. Each institution, home, career, sports, and religion, is something to which individuals are exposed in varying degrees. Thus, a child who regularly attends church will be more exposed to **several** attitudes, e.g., belief in God, the singing of hymns, the giving of charity, etc., than one who does not, and will thus finish at a higher level by conditioning on **all** of them. This would account for the resulting appearance of the attitude loading pattern as a single factor.

2. A sem can appear as an adjunct to an existing well-learned factor, partaking of a uniform motivation therefore in the learning of the elements of the second factor. For example, a person of delicate health may learn more about all vitamins than another or a person with scientific interests may decide that he needs to read easily in German and in time acquires a pattern of attitudes around the German language sem.

3. In Piaget's studies of cognitive development, he recognizes what we may call **aids** (Cattell, 1971). These are breakthroughs in thinking in which some discovery is made that suddenly has many applications. For example, a child perceives the nature of causality or of the similatities of algebra and geometry and then comes rapidly to gain intellectual control of a whole set of ideas. A parallel process to this also can occur in the affective realm and lead to rapid simultaneous learning of a whole set of attitudes dependent on the insight. For example, a child may realize how much what is learned at school is applicable to life and

thus acquire a heightened interest in all that has to do with school, an increase in the school sentiment.

Most sentiments have something that can be called **an object** without which a whole set of sem attitudes would be devoid of satisfaction. Something like this happens when a person gets a religious conversion or suddenly grasps the real objectives of a certain career.

It is, of course, impossible to describe the rise of sentiments in terms of standard, reflexological Pavlovian-Skinnerian concepts because the human mind is forever linking up this and that by **spontaneous thought**, but the production of a sentiment structure comes near to reflexological concepts in what we may call the **common learning schedule** case above. The second, which we may call **budding**, and the third, which we may call **inherent agency** growth require the fuller concepts of what we designate below as structured learning theory.

It would not be surprising to developing theory to find as we do that dR-technique experiments plainly show the same ergic factor patterns as R-technique; but it is, perhaps, surprising to find that the factoring of difference scores, differences in the same people between two occasions, actually show essentially the same **semic** patterns. That is to say, the attitude elements in a sem rise and fall together. In the case of ergs this functional unity has been shown by experiments on the fear and sex ergs in which stimuli have been applied of a nature expected to arouse the erg (Cattell, 1973; Cattell & Barton, 1974; Cattell, Kawash, & DeYoung, 1972; DeYoung & Horn, 1974; Krug, 1977) and have done so significantly. Thus Krug (1977) and Dunfor (1985) found that the U component in fear rose on other attitudes than that stimulated. Krug found that a *frustrating* stimulus to a sem (to school) cut down all T scores on the unitary sentiment. The unitary activations level concept is thus supported.

In the case of sems experiment lags behind concepts, and there are few experiments showing that when certain attitudes in a sem are roused by stimulation to higher levels the other attitudes in the sem rise with them (Krug, 1971, 1977; DeYoung et al., 1973). The functional unity of sems needs more experimental investigation; but the evidence suggests that there is a **network of cognitive associations** across the domain of a given erg, such that stimulation runs across it, tending to activate all elements. If you say "Washington" to a patriotic American in the next few minutes, he is likely to remember more readily "crossing the Delaware." We call this rise in strength of all attitudes in a sem its **activation**, which we distinguish from the more affective physiological **arousal** of a unitary erg.

7   Preliminary Calculations on Decision, Conflict, and the Strength of Sems

It behooves us next to look at the interactions of ergs and sems, in the phenomena we call decision, conflict, suppression, and control. If it is true that in deciding between two courses of action that with stronger impulse wins out, then we can use the two behavioral equations to predict the nature of a decision.

Let the equations be (7–1a) and (7–b) below.

$$a_{hijk} = \overset{x=m}{\sum} b_{hjkx} E_{xi} + \overset{y=n}{\sum} b_{hjky} M_{yi} \qquad (7\text{–}1a)$$

$$a_{hipk} = \overset{x=m}{\sum} b_{hpk} E_{xi} + \overset{y=n}{\sum} b_{hpk} M_{yi} \qquad (7\text{–}1b)$$

Then if the loadings in Equation (7–1a) are greater than Equation (7–b)—the E's and M's being those of the same person—the decision will go to Equation (7–1a) because a_{hijk} will be larger than a_{hipk}, h, j and p being the alternative courses of response to hk.

However, turning next to the experience of conflict in a decision, it is clear that conflict is likely to be greater if a_{hijk} and a_{hipk} are closer in strength and also if both urges are stronger. Thus, the first, most likely measure of conflict, c_{jp}, will be

$$c_{jpi} = \frac{a_{hijk} + a_{hipk}}{a_{hijk} - a_{hipk}} \qquad (7\text{–}2)$$

We may speak of such conflict as **active** conflict because at the given moment the individual is actively deciding between j and p responses in attitudes in response to his life stimulus situation.

A study of **means for measuring conflict independent** of the above as a criterion was carried out by Cattell and Sweney (1964), who took 24 accepted signs of conflict such as: vacillating in decision, interference with attention and memory, anxiety expressions, and attempts at suppression. These were measured on 127 children on different loci (sociological) and foci (among inner structures) and revealed eight factors, named as follows:

1. suppressive action with cognitive disturbances
2. restriction of the ego, of area of action
3. fantasy in frustration
4. ignoring problem (versus ego action)
5. tension and increased impulsivity
6., 7., and 8. less defined, no titles given.

The overall research plan was to relate active conflict magnitudes by Equation (7–1a) and (7–1b) to measures of these conflict signs, but this remains incomplete.

Meanwhile we must recognize in contrast to **active**, overt conflict the **indurated**, often unconscious conflict among underlying drives which remains after some compromise has been reached among the alternatives considered in active conflict. This conflict is revealed by the magnitude of negative loadings when the behavioral equation is found for a course of life action to which a person has become reconciled. For example, as Lawlis (1971) shows, the interest in having a job in a group half unemployed was as follows (simplified by omissions of less significant factors):

$$Job = 0.38M_1 + 0.21M_2 - 0.12E_1 + 0.35E_2 - 0.16E_3 \qquad (7\text{–}3)$$

Here M_1 is career sentiment, M_2 is home sentiment, E_1 is pugnacity, E_2 is sex, and E_3 is fear. We conclude that the satisfaction in working lies in the career, in sex, and in the home sentiment, but that two ergs, pugnacity and fear, are actually thwarted by this course of action as shown by the negative signs. The negative signs mean that as the job is done more earnestly, the expression of pugnacity and the need for

TABLE 7-1. Dynamic Factor Structure as a Basis for Calculating Ergic Involvement of any Sem (Strength of a Sem)

Evidence for the dynamic factor structure

Attitudes	Factors (pattern)										
I want:	Fear	Mating	Assertiveness	Narcism	Pugnacity	Self-sentiment	Superego	Career	Sweetheart	Home-parental	Residual
1. Protection from A-bomb	55	-18	-32	-06	45	00	-17	10	-13	16	-26
2. To avoid disease, injury	84	-01	-21	16	-20	-16	12	20	04	-12	-15
3. To fall in love	04	68	11	09	10	09	11	-28	-18	07	06
4. To satisy sexual needs	-06	60	12	08	-14	-06	-10	08	03	-38	-01
5. To dress smartly	-18	01	67	25	-21	-23	03	-29	-21	29	06
6. To increase salary, status	24	17	47	16	-28	16	02	32	-16	-30	-06
7. to enjoy delicacies	62	-20	16	58	10	14	-00	03	11	-05	19
8. To rest, have easy time	-13	-01	47	24	31	43	-07	-20	17	-35	38
9. To destroy our enemies	-07	-20	17	05	80	-06	14	04	07	-07	-00
10. To see violent movies	-02	25	-23	55	38	-22	-05	-00	02	-21	-09
11. To control impulses	32	-07	-05	-12	14	42	31	-29	09	-06	-59
12. Never to damage self-respect	-10	-11	-08	17	-13	90	-06	16	11	08	04

13. To maintain reputation	-22	-34	03	42	-29	58	26	-04	-29	01	-12
14. Never to be insane	05	23	-6	09	14	84	30	06	-04	15	-15
15. A normal sexual adjustment	17	55	02	-07	22	47	-04	28	25	19	10
16. To know myself better	44	13	01	-04	-09	43	10	-18	06	09	18
17. To look after family	23	-19	-08	-02	-00	16	01	-08	-04	36	71
18. To be proficient in career	37	10	69	11	22	45	-12	19	-04	36	71
19. To satisfy sense of duty	06	-21	19	-15	-15	-08	61	25	23	-10	-41
20. To end all vice	-07	17	-68	-18	-00	34	55	17	-09	-03	19
21. To be unselfish	-04	06	19	-01	10	02	73	-03	10	10	12
22. to avoid impropriety	05	19	-27	09	-17	-04	82	-10	-11	23	-18
23. To learn my job well	04	02	25	17	00	08	04	79	-05	-03	07
24. To stick with my job	13	05	-15	-61	-11	-11	35	58	-03	-16	07
25. to spend time with sweetheart	-05	-11	-11	11	00	-01	-02	-07	83	13	06
26. To bring gifts to sweetheart	03	12	10	-06	01	-00	01	01	83	12	-09
27. My parents to be proud	-11	09	28	-01	-03	26	01	04	08	80	-06
28. To depend on my parents	10	-00	09	-20	-23	-00	-05	-05	-00	87	09

Source: adapted from Cattell, Horn, and Butcher (1962) for the Motivation Analysis Test Handbook (1964).

security are reduced. We discuss an alternative possible interpretation of this sign elsewhere, but the most likely is that given: as these two needs increase, the desire for the job decreases.

In indurated job conflict we thus have a built-in situation in which some ergic conflict **has** to occur due to circumstances as a condition of following up the best compromise solution that can be found by the individuals concerned. There is thus a cancellation of some of the satisfaction of the positively loaded ergs and sems by that of those negatively loaded. Granted equal value for different ergs we can calculate the magnitude of conflict as a percentage (from Equation 7–3):

$$c = \frac{0.11 + 0.16}{0.38 + 0.28 + 0.11 + 0.16 + 0.35} = 0.24 \qquad (7\text{-}4a)$$

or in general terms,

$$c_{bjk} = \frac{\Sigma \bar{b}_{bjk}}{\Sigma \bar{b}_{bjk} + \Sigma \overset{+}{b}_{bjk}} \qquad (7\text{-}4b)$$

where a sign over the b's indicates a sum of all those values with that sign. (Incidentally, instead of taking the denominator as the **total** dynamic index loading, we could take only the positive; but the present is logically better.)

If we now took **all** of a person's attitudes and compounded the result in Equation (7–4b), we should have an index of the **total** conflict which each person has been so unfortunate as to build into life. This totality cannot be actually calculated—it is too vast—but we **can** compare people on a standard representative sample of attitudes from important life areas. The **integration** level of a personality may well be defined as the obverse of such a total conflict measure thus:

$$I = \frac{\Sigma \bar{b} + \Sigma \overset{+}{b}}{\Sigma \bar{b}} = \frac{1}{\Sigma c} \qquad (7\text{-}4c)$$

(or as I–C to keep I below unity.)

As a check on the psychological reality of such an objective index Williams (1959) calculated I for a small number of psychotic individuals in mental hospitals and a corresponding number of normals and found a significant difference in the expected direction. Because the factorings had to be by P-technique (since the b's here must be peculiar to the individual), he used only a small number of cases, and no one has yet repeated this crucial experiment. Consequently, until confirmed, the theory of so measuring integration must remain unsupported but this concept within the **dynamic calculus** is an important one with great practical clinical and general relevance.

A third approach to measuring conflict—beyond calculating c or getting a direct measure by summing the Sweney conflict factors—is by contrasting U and I measures in the given area. As Heather Cattell (1984) finds clinically, however, there is a catch in equating (U minus I) to conflict. Although usually the unintegrated excess shows an obstruction or an incapacity in obtaining an expression in the given area, when very low, it may also indicate that the individual has invested his needs very fully in suitable expressions and has then experienced a physiological subsidence of the need in age. It is the case of the old man esthetically interested in chorus girls and bawdy displays. In any case we do not yet have experimental comparisons to clarify relationships of the three modes of measuring conflict, but clinical and social psychology would obviously benefit from a firm comparison of their forms.

The next calculation of value in this area is that of what we may call the strength of a sem in terms of the particular ergs that obtain satisfaction through it and support it. We shall speak of **the ergic investment in a sem** and recognize that in everyday life we note that some sems are much stronger than others, e.g., that to the family is commonly stronger than that to a hobby.

The calculation is complicated by the fact that in any dynamic lattice a sem subsidiates not only ultimately to ergic goals but to other sems in between. (The second mode of arising of sems, the budding origin above, would lead us to expect a fair amount of this sequential use of ergic forces. It is like several water mills in a stream utilizing in succession the same flow of water—to pursue our hydraulic model). Consequently, when we look at a dynamic factor analytic matrix, we may expect the same erg to load appreciably on the same attitude as is loaded on several sems. Table 7-1 shows the loadings of the five sentiment factors in the MAT on ergic factors. The loadings tend to be small because most of the variances on these specially selected attitudes are chosen for high semic loadings. We can see that the sem to the parents has some loading in self-assertion (proud of the parents) and willingness to sacrifice narcism and pugnacity (negative loadings). The two attitudes' loading and marking careers have different ergic investments, which we must expect to find, but the total is negative of narcism, which must be sacrificed, e.g., in getting up early in the morning, and positive on need for security and self-assertion. The many attitudes marking the self-sentiment add up positively on narcism, assertiveness, sex, and need for security—especially the last. The special properties of the self-sentiment will be discussed in the next chapter, but in it and the other sems we can recognize that the ergs loaded are those we should expect to support the sem. The question is how we can calculate the amount of investment of the ergs in a given sem.

The **behavioral indices**, b's, state the **rate of increase** of the one—the dependent variable—with a unit increase in the other. The role of the factor in the sem seems best assessed as the product of the loading on the sem with the loading of the attitude on the erg. Thus, in Table 7–1 the attitude "To learn my job well" would contribute $0.25 \times 0.79 = 0.20$ of assertiveness to the career sentiment. By adding over half a dozen prominent career attitudes, for example, we would reach the total ergic involvement, with allowance for intercorrelation of attitudes. Because of the subsidiation of sems sometimes to one another, the total ergic investment in a sem would not be expected to retain a meaningful upper limit in relation to another sem, but the ergic involvement would indicate the strength of a sem, its role in decision making, etc.

8   The Three Internal Factors in the Social Control of Behavior

It has been said that a person with much semic development is more stable than one whose whole dynamics runs only to ergic expressions. This is true only within a culture in which the sems develop, for the behavior of a purely ergic personality is quite predictable. The person will react dependably to whatever the ergs are innately set to respond to. In the citizen with considerable semic development the behavior will appear to other citizens to be more dependable, because he will react in ways much better fitted to the culture. The sems have drained off much impulsive energy resident in the ergs into ways that the culture has found to be more adapted and also useful to others.

The mere existence of sems is by no means the whole story of control. The individual controls antisocial behavior from both ergs and sems by virtue of the rise of the ego, and self-sentiment, and the superego. The latter two are measurable by both objective motivation tests (MAT and SMAT) and by questionnaire and other personality tests, but the ego (as factor C in the 16 PF, HSPQ (High School Personality Questionnaire), CPQ (Child Personality Questionnaire), etc.) is measured so far only by personality measures.

Let us first briefly consider their nature as shown by loading patterns. The superego is essentially as Freud saw it: a set of attitudes directed to moral behavior. As Table 7–1 shows, duty, opposition to vice, unselfishness, and control of improper behavior are central. The self-sentiment, by contrast, is a pattern not seen by Freud and most clinicians. It is concerned with maintaining the social acceptability of the self and, indeed, even its physical existence. The loaded attitudes are to control impulse, to maintain social reputation, to be sane, to be normal in sex, and to know our nature better. They concern "self esteem."

39

The theory of the self-sentiment is that it subsidiates to most other satisfactions, so that its maintenance as respectable is seen as a condition of obtaining most other ends in society. It concerns itself with both the physical and the psychological, social well-being, centering on a cognitive concept of the self. By some observers it is called self esteem or self concept, etc.; but experimentally it is a clearcut sem factor in objective motivation measures and in questionnaires (Q_3). It associates itself with better school performance, reduced general anxiety, freedom from delinquency, and leadership (Cattell, Eber, & Tatsuoka, 1970). As a cooperative factor it includes loadings on some attitudes that enter the superego and to some extent subsidiates to the maintenance of the superego factor.

The third factor in the directive, control set of factors is the ego, mainly located in personality factoring as C. It has essentially the characteristics described by Freud. It scores very low in neurosis, psychosis, and most forms of pathology. It has a large negative role in anxiety. It is independent of the self-sentiment, Q_3, and the superego, G, though these two are regularly positively mutually correlated—they form a second order factor, along with desurgency, F −, called control, believed due to good upbringing. C is not moral: it controls simply in the interests of greatetst overall satisfaction to the given individual. The low C person has poor control of impulses and moods, feels that life goes wrong, lacks persistence, and is anxious and wayward.

In resisting a temptation that would lead us into trouble, all three of these controlling structures tend to play a part. If a_{hjk} were a foolish act in terms of long-term goals, we should expect a behavioral equation for it as follows:

$$a_{hijk} = \sum^{x=p} b_{hikx} E_{xi} + \sum^{y=q} b_{hjky} M_{yi} - b_{hjkc} C_i - b_{hjkg} G_i$$

$$- b_{hjk\,3} Q_{3i} \qquad (8\text{-}1)$$

The stronger the measures on C, G, and Q_3, therefore, the more inhibition we should expect. The natures of G and Q_3 need little further discussion. G has relatively little heredity in it and derives from education, though the need for self-esteem, Q_3, has more than one might expect (Cattell, 1982). G is built up largely within the family, depending on early introjection of the standards brought to bear by beloved parents as Freud and others have argued. Fear of loss of parental love is its central motivation, and guilt is the experience of denying its injunctions.

Whereas G rests on deeper, more archaic sems, Q_3 deals more with social values and manners. This can be seen in the correlating attitudes. Default on G's demands leads to guilt, but on Q_3's social demands, to shame. The projections on the frontal lobes of the cortex operate in both but particularly in guilt. The superego has a significant correlation with interest in religion, Q_3 in the population generally. Inasmuch as most people keep out of the hands of the police we must suppose that these two factors are large, relative to most other sems and ergs, and able to outweigh combinations of the dynamic structures in an equation like (8-1). In average age plots both show an upward growth from early adolescence into middle age.

Like G and Q_3 the structure of the ego is more complex than that of all ordinary sems. It grows by success in control, gaining reinforcement each time it controls an impulse to give more reward in the long run. It has its resemblance to an ability, therefore, and its life course is highly similar to that of crystallized intelligence; g_c.

We can analyze the skills that the ego needs to develop into four steps as follows:

1. Evaluating strength of dynamic needs. This involves directly sensing how strong various ergs and sentiments are in competitively calling for expression. It is performed partly by (a) direct sensitivity and (b) by cue evocation of traits, CET, i.e., by setting up imaginary stimuli to incite drives. Unconsciousness of some drives balks this operation.
2. Evaluating the probabilities in the external situation. This involves much intelligence and experience of the outcome of earlier behaviors. It calls for emotional realism and correct retrieval from memory of previous outcomes to be weighed.
3. Producing a decision. This requires (a) control by inhibition of thrusting impulses long enough to permit deliberation and (b) decision on the basis of information in steps 1 and 2 above.
4. Effective implementation of the decision. In the face of opposing forces the g implementation calls for two effectors, (a) the sheer weight of the ego sentiment itself as developed to this point and (b) the management of cues by CET skills to evoke by the modulation of the *right* dynamic trains the allies suitable for the given struggle.

The first step above, deciding whether one is hungry or tired, for example, may be aided by words and experience. The second step may look like a task of sheer intelligence, but we find virtually no correlation of C and B (intelligence); and we must conclude that the main task is overcoming emotional obstacles. In the third step we would put more weight on the sheer capacity to say "Halt!" while deliberation occurs. C factor has an appreciable (about 50 percent) hereditary determination, and it is probably here in the sheer capacity to control that this plays its part. In *The Young Delinquent* Burt (1927) stresses an apparently hereditary capacity to control "general emotionality," which could be what operates here. Without this halt to the immediate rise of impulse, the other capacities cannot have occasion to operate.

Finally, we cannot overlook step 4, putting the decision into action, for introspections often show all going well up to the decision but failure thereafter. In step 4(b) this mainly involves an activity of the imagination in stirring up the ergs and sems that would be likely to oppose the course of action that needs to be inhibited. Here we step fairly soon into the last-ditch defenses of psychoanalysis in which repression, fantasy, projection, and other resources are finally used to stabilize the opposition to behavior. These defenses tend to leave permanent effects if resorted to too severely.

9   The Dynamic Equations
of Personality Learning

So far our concern has been to get perspective on structure as it exists. This has been put on a firm foundation by broadly conceived factor analytic studies. From this point on, however, with dependence on more intermittent patches of experimental work we advance more speculatively to changes with time.

The reflexological learning theory, from Pavlov through Skinner, has produced good scientific laws regarding the acquisition of specific responses; but we have to move on to **structured learning theory** to find out (a) how complex personality **traits** are acquired and (b) how existing personality traits enter into the prediction of learning.

The first condition to be kept in mind is that all learning is **multidimensional change in a multidimensional situation**—most of which has been ruled out in reflexological learning experiments. Let us first systematize, however, what happens in a dynamic learning experience, presented by adjustment process analysis. Basically what we have is an individual starting out to satisfy a desire and encountering various situations which modify that desire. The possible outcomes are shown in the Adjustment Process Analysis (*APA*) chart in Figure 9–1. The subject proceeds through a series of *choice points* at each of which some solutions end his pilgrimage if possible, but which pursued to ultimate frustration end in pathological responses. The *APA* chart has clinical use in diagnosis and in communication about the stage of a case to another practitioner by symbols A_1, B_2, C_1, etc., indicating the arrest point.

To find out what experience of each path does to a personality trait, we have to first start out empirically in a relatively blind fashion.

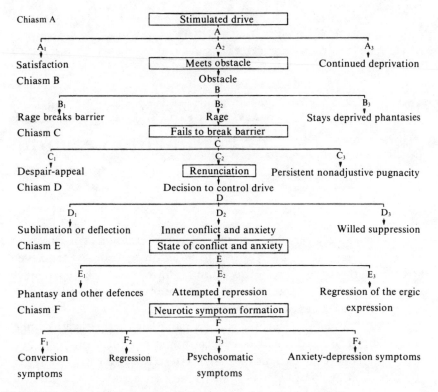

FIGURE 9–1. The adjustment process analysis (APA) chart.

With living people in a moving world we cannot hold all else constant to see what a particular experience does as in a rat experiment. We must accept the multidimensional world and tease out by more subtle multivariate analysis the effects of features of the life situation upon traits that will be changing simultaneously.

Our first design for this purpose is called the Learning Summary Matrix Method for Path Learning Analysis (PLA). It takes several people, who are following various paths simultaneously in their lives, to varying degrees, and measures the changes in their personality traits. Matrix analysis finds from this data what one experience of a path does to all personality traits. In Figure 9–2 the first matrix, L, is called the Learning Law Matrix because it contains the desired information of what personality changes follow from experience of each path. A path is defined as, for example, going to college for a year; getting married;

holding a given job for a year, etc. We suppose that in our group of subjects we can write up a second matrix, E, the experience matrix, in which figures tell us how much experience each person has of each path.

If we multiply the law matrix by the experience matrix, we shall know how much change to expect in each person's traits. This occurs because of the laws of matrix multiplication. We multiply a row in the first matrix by a *column* in the second matrix; thus, we should take trait A_1 from L and multiply by the column for person, P_I, from matrix E. This might give products as follows:

$$\alpha_1 (0.12 \times 2) + \alpha_2 (-0.30 \times 1) + \alpha_3 (0.25 \times 2) = 0.19 \quad (9-1)$$

The answer—.44—is the sum of the three products in each of which we multiply what happens through one transit of a path by how much or how many times the given person (one group in Figure 9-2) has passed along it. This answer is placed in the upper left corner of the personality change matrix, shown on the right in Figure 9-2.

Now we do not have the Learning Law Matrix. This is what we are out to find, but we do have the account of path experiences and the change in the personality factors for each person to go in the right-hand matrix. With a computer and these two matrices we can work out the L matrix as shown in the equation at the bottom. (We must leave the student to find the laws for handling matrix calculation, e.g., in Child (1970); Cattell (1978); Horst (1963); or Gorsuch (1974).)

What we have done here is reach a result about traversing a life path without having to control every subject's life so that only that one path is traversed. We have done so, it is true, at the cost of considering learning defined by a multiplication operation: what a path does multiplied by the number of traverses. That is a fairly reasonable assumption. From it we have emerged with a finding of use in clinical, social, and developmental areas of psychology; namely, how much a single experience of a given life path typically alters a person's personality trait scores. Some first findings on this are given by Barton and Cattell (1972a; 1972b), and others. For example, holding down a job increases the dominance, E factor score; falling severely ill reduces C, and raises I, O, Q_4, and the second order anxiety and cortertia factor scores.

In the ordinary, classical plots of learning curves we plot successive scores on an a_{hjk} measure, as in countless reflexological studies with animals. But learning is more than this; it is, for example, a change in *the way* a person achieves a score, e.g., in what different abilities he brings to bear. A change could occur in the behavioral indices, the b's, in Equation (7-1) (p.IPR) as well as in a_{hijk} and the trait scores. In fact, Fleishman (1967) showed long ago that in ability performances the involvement of the principal primary abilities continually changes as a group goes on practicing. For example, more intelligence may be involved at the beginning and more visual acuity later on.

The same is true of personality and motivational behavior. We can get at the b changes by a matrix experiment very similar to that just examined except that we now enter with groups instead of individuals as shown in Figure 9-2, shown by groups instead of individuals in E. Here by inversion of a matrix, shown in the bottom equation, we solve for the learning law matrix, L, which tells us how repetition of the paths changes the b's.

It may be objected that though T and b changes by paths are helpful knowledge for clinical and developmental psychology, it is still gross in

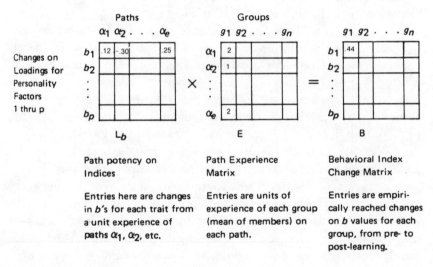

The solution for learning relation law matrix, L_b, is:

$$L_b = B\,E'\,(E\,E')^{-1},\ \text{as given in (9-1) in the text}$$

Since obtaining behavioral indices requires a factor analysis we have either to compare R-technique results on groups, or P-technique results at different intervals of learning process progress in an individual. (These stages would replace g_1, g_2, etc., in E above.)

FIGURE 9-2. Path learning analysis method of calculating learning changes in the behavioral indices—b's.

that it tells us **what** a given path does but not *why* it does so. It does not tell us about the reward effects in the path, or its degree of complexity, or the effects of frustrations.

It is possible, however, by further steps to proceed to find the effects and potencies of these determiners in paths as follows. First, we must find means of scoring paths for these determiners; these scores can be in any units we like but must be definite enough for any scorer to recognize.

We start off now with a prior scoring of each path on a list of determiners, as in the middle of Figure 9-3, where each figure represents how much that determiner occurs in the path. The middle matrix simply records how many or how powerful the determiners are recorded to be in the given path. On the right we look for the power of each determiner as it contributes to the learning in each path and on the left the matrix of unknown determiner potencies that we wish to find out. This has been called the **Determiner Potency Analysis** (*DPA*) experiment with solution as shown by:

$$PD = L \qquad\qquad\qquad (9\text{-}2)$$

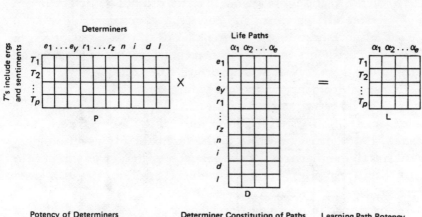

Potency of Determiners	Determiner Constitution of Paths	Learning Path Potency
Entries are mean effect of a unit increase in the given determiner on mean size of measured trait change (mean of a group is used).	Entries are endowments of the given unit path in the "teaching properties," e, ergic tension, r, reward, etc. over all ergs. D describes what one expects to meet.	Entries are mean trait change, calculated for unit experience of the given path.

FIGURE 9-3. Determiner potency analysis (DPA). The discovery of potencies of constituent determiners in a path.

The analysis is for a single life[1] path.

Step 1 in Calculation: Trait Change from Each Dynamic Trait's Fate

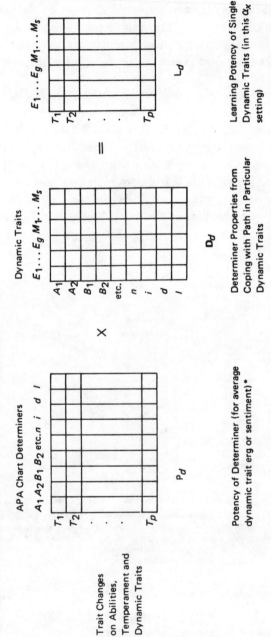

Trait Changes
on Abilities,
Temperament and
Dynamic Traits

P_d

Potency of Determiner (for average dynamic trait erg or sentiment) *

D_d

Determiner Properties from Coping with Path in Particular Dynamic Traits

L_d

Learning Potency of Single Dynamic Traits (in this α_x setting)

*It may prove desirable to average separately for ergs and sentiments, in which case D would have only one class of entry, E's or M's.

[1]It is important here to distinguish between the life paths which are α's here, and the APA chart incidents which are things happening in the course of life paths as analyzed in APA terms. Thus rather than think of a path itself producing effects on traits we refer now to

FIGURE 9-4(a). The learning effect of a particular dynamic trait strength

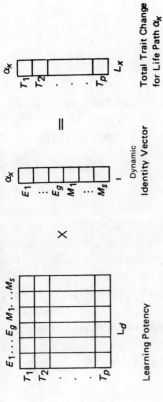

Step 2 in Calculation. Total Trait Change for Path α_x

$$
\begin{array}{c}
\overset{\displaystyle E_1 \ldots E_g \; M_1 \ldots M_s}{
\begin{array}{c}
T_1 \\ T_2 \\ \cdot \\ \cdot \\ T_p
\end{array}
}
\\
L_d
\end{array}
\times
\begin{array}{c}
\overset{\displaystyle \alpha_x}{
\begin{array}{c}
E_1 \\ \vdots \\ E_g \\ M_1 \\ \vdots \\ M_s
\end{array}
}
\\
\end{array}
=
\begin{array}{c}
\overset{\displaystyle \alpha_x}{
\begin{array}{c}
T_1 \\ T_2 \\ \cdot \\ \cdot \\ T_p
\end{array}
}
\\
L_x
\end{array}
$$

Learning Potency

by Dynamic Traits in Path α_x

Dynamic Identity Vector

Total Trait Change for Life Path α_x

Step 3 in Calculation: Assembling Results in Terms of *e* life paths

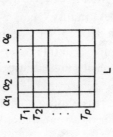

$$
\begin{array}{c}
\overset{\displaystyle \alpha_1 \; \alpha_2 \ldots \alpha_e}{
\begin{array}{c}
T_1 \\ T_2 \\ \cdot \cdot \cdot \\ T_p
\end{array}
}
\\
L
\end{array}
$$

Learning Path Potency, as in Figure 9-3

Determiner potency analysis with assumption of specificity to dynamic traits (DPA·DS)

FIGURE 9-4(b). The final effect of particular path dynamics

49

However, if we wish to derive from the *PLA* equations *L, E,* and *B* (no longer for groups) earlier, this becomes:

$$PDE = T \qquad\qquad (9\text{--}3)$$

where *T* equals trait changes. From this the backward calculation to get the P matrix of potency of determiners on traits is carried out by:

$$P = TE^{-1}D^{-1} \qquad\qquad (9\text{--}4)$$

using what is called the generalized inverse calculation $E^{-1} = E'(EE')^{-1}$ from equation (9–2).

One further refinement is possible beyond Figure 9–3 if we care to assume that the effect of the determiner is specific to each dynamic trait—as in fact is very likely. In that case we have a three-step matrix calculation as shown in Figure 9–4. Step two here is only a device for rearranging the results for the final overview of what each path does to each trait, as in:

$$P_{d1} = L_{d1}D'_{d1}(D_{d1}D'_{d1})^{-1} \qquad\qquad (9\text{--}5)$$

where footnote 1 indicates the action of a particular dynamic trait, 1.

The matrix calculations here have not yet been applied by anyone to gathered data. However, they present the first actual solutions to the problem of personality changes on measured unitary personality traits under explicit determiners. In the *APA*, the *PLA* for behavioral indices, and the *DPA* for general and specific traits this chapter offers a way to calculate the basic rules about the effects on traits of specific life paths and of specific determiners in those paths. By this means we can test the theory of the three modes of development of sems in Chapter 8 and reach conclusions about structured learning in broad personality traits of all kinds.

10

The Unfolding
of Behavioral Sequences

What we have studied so far gives us structure and the basic changes of structure with experience of learning. However, we recognize that personality is more than a structure. It is a **process** going on from birth to death, with the understanding and prediction of its action depending on dynamic moments additional to structure. In this chapter we shall attempt the difficult task of following how a dynamic structure results in a purposive, adjustive flow of behavior.

Our analysis will apply either to an erg or a sem but naturally with more emphasis on acquired elements in the latter. For relative simplicity let us take an intelligent mammal such as a flesh-eating, hunting lion, who is on the path of seeking prey at a water hole. We observe here what is essentially a part of the dynamic lattice laid out in time with behavior subsidiating fairly directly to an ergic goal. In passing let us note that in the human dynamic lattice, though the latter subgoals, nearer to the ergic goal, necessarily **follow** achievement of the earlier goals, the actual time sequence of work on the various paths need not follow a temporal order. For example, supplying a bank balance subsidiates to spending the money in it on the home, but a person may actually spend some of the money on Monday and arrange to work to recoup the loss on Tuesday.

With the proviso that the temporal order is not always the order in the lattice, let us, however, take an animal example in which the two orders happen more simply to be the same. Our task is to explain on conditioning principles, with the aid of structured learning facts, the phenomenon of **pursuit of a goal with varied responsiveness according to circumstances**. The chain reflex explanation does not account for the adaptiveness to new situations that an animal encounters in pursuing a goal. A model with new features is needed. The lion is impelled by hunger to go to the water hole where he has waylaid food before. This is represented in Figure 10–1 by an arrow sign as $k_o h_I$ (k for the internal hunger situation, h for a stimulus to move), which would represent a number of b's in the behavioral equation for that behavior, all with the same subscripts.

On reaching the water hole, marked as subgoal, SG_I, the animal has the choice of rushing out at once or hiding in the undergrowth. The

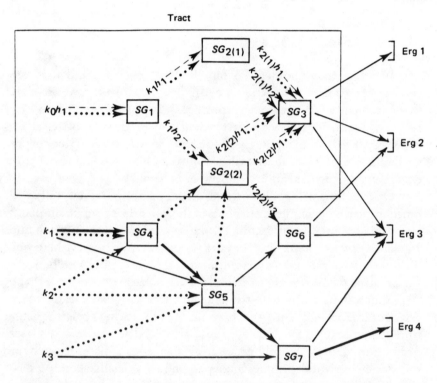

Three kinds of abstractions are illustrated in this dynamic lattice. (1) A simple tandem *chain* from k_1 to Erg 4, by the heavy line ⸻ (2) A *sentiment* structure with the goal, subgoal SG_3, running from k_0, k_1, k_2, and k_3 the courses in which are shown by .... arrows. (3) A *tract* beginning at k_0 and ending at SG_3, shown by -------- lines. The remaining courses, e.g., those ending in the four ergs, are in simple lines.

The sequences are shown in detail only in the tract. The subgoals are there numbered in order 1, 2, and 3, and the ambient situation k created by each is similarly numbered. At ambient situations k_1 and k_2 are there in each case two stimuli, h_1 and h_2, one of which will be paramount on any one occasion.

FIGURE 10–1. Illustrating by anxiety the essence of modulation theory.

lion's choice is determined by the relative strength of two new situations and stimuli, k_1h_1 and k_1h_2, representing the number of prey in view and the amount of cover in the underbrush.

Let us keep here to Tract 1 in Figure 10-1, the portion in a rectangle which is actually linked in the total dynamic structure to other tracts, beginning with other internal and external situations, k_1, k_2, and k_3. In Tract 1 the choice at SG_1 will lead to either $SG_{2(1)}$ or $SG_{2(2)}$. At each of these a new decision has to be made. If we suppose $k_{2(2)}h_2$ is a stronger stimulus than $k_{2(1)}h_1$ then the animal may have singled out a particuar zebra and begun to approach it. At this point, SG_2, the lion sees the zebra beginning to run, $k_{2(1)}h_2$, and is impelled to run and spring. Thus, he attains SG_3, the kill, which subsidiates to erg 1 of hunger and, in a larger diagram, to ergs 2 and 3 which represent self-assertive status as well as the need to feed the cubs.

This account differs from a learned chain reflex (illustrated in Figure 10-1 by a thick line from k_1 to erg_4) in the reaction to different stimulus-situation at each subgoal, and the effect of changing ergic tension. The relative power of these stimuli depends on their relative prominence and on the accumulations of the result of past experiences in reacting to them. The persistence to a desired goal with varied effort on different occasions is thus accounted for both by an expected appearance of new stimuli at subgoals and by the animal's possession of reactivities to these stimuli—in this case largely innate reactivities.

The absence of either component can bring the process to an abortive end. If there is no prey at the pool, the process stops, and if the lion lacks reactivity to the zebra's running away, the process ends. The process is therefore guaranteed to be adaptive to inner and outer circumstances. If the right circumstances appear it will inevitably move to the desired ergic goal by different alternative paths. Without these alternative reactivities in the animal we would have only a chain reflex of exactly prescribed sequences that would be incomplete and much more frequent.

Each path in Figure 10-1 can be represented by a behavioral equation, (with the new h and perhaps by a new k) if there is change in the internal state. The decision at each subgoal is effected by comparison of the strengths from the equations, as in Equation (7-1) (p. 32) above. Thus, the attitudes that correlate to form a sem or an erg may either be parallel as in Figure 3-1 (p. 14) or sequential; since in general there will be approximately equal strength in attitudes that subsidiate one to another.

In fact, we are now saying that each ergic or semic factor is not only defined as a structure **but also as an unfolding process**. Its form can in theory be recognized as a unitary entity from either observational approach, though the process approach offers a less simple way of reaching quantitative loadings, etc. than the cross-sectional factoring of attitudes.

At this point also we must begin to recognize that the behavioral index, b, as a factor loading, is actually a more complex value than it seems. The study of modulation of states accustoms us to the idea of a modulating index, s_{kx} operating upon a state liability, L_{xi}, to produce the observed state level of an individual in a certain circumstance, k, thus:

$$S_{xik} = s_{kx} L_{xi} \qquad (10\text{-}1)$$

Since we know that a state produces a change in behavior a_{hijk}, according to its loading that we will now write v_{hjk} for the *involvement* of the state in the given behavior, we have:

$$a_{hijk} = v_{hjkx} S_{xik} = v_{hjkx} s_{kx} L_{xi} \qquad (10\text{-}2)$$

It will be seen that in a factoring which reaches L_x as a trait, as a liability or proneness to the emotion, x, then:

$$v_{hjkx} s_{kx} = b_{hjkx} \qquad (10\text{-}3)$$

i.e., as far as a trait of liability to a state is concerned, L_x, the loading, b_x, can be broken down into an involvement index, v_x, and a modulator index, s_{kx}. The latter, as we know from modulator theory, states for the average person how much a certain situation will evoke a certain state. For example, as far as liability to fear or anxiety is concerned, s_f will be large for being caught in a house on fire and small for lazing on a holiday beach.

Cattell and Brennan (1984) have tried out the modulation model for the states of depression and of anxiety and have shown (Figure 10-2) that it holds well for these states. That is to say, if we have scores for a high and a low liability group in depression and then take state scores on those groups at some intermediate provocation of depression, the two points will be found to fit on the lines joining the high and low to the goodness of fit revealed in Figure 10-2.

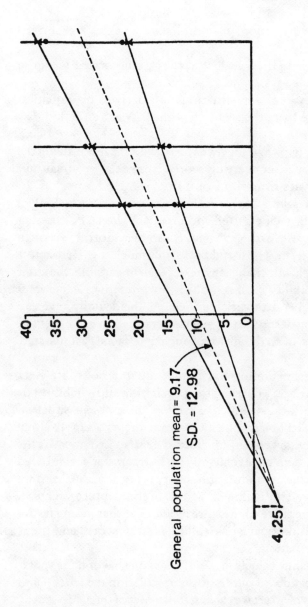

General population mean = 9.17
S.D. = 12.98

4.25

• = Actual point
x = Point on best fitting line

FIGURE 10-2.   Illustrating by anxiety the essence of modulation theory.

55

More is implied by this finding than immediately meets the eye. It operates with two scales, one for the **state** scores and one for the s_k values of various life situations. It supposes:

1. That state provocation, s_k, x and state level, S_x, reach zero simultaneously.
2. That this zero on the S scale is a true zero no matter what the raw score scale says.
3. That the s_k values for situations are derived by Equation (10–1) above from the real state scores at each situation.

For the first time in psychology we thus have a means of fixing the true zeros on state scales, converting scores from relative equal unit scales to true, ratio scales from three or more measures.

There are other features of this scaling system that can be looked into elsewhere (Cattell, 1958; Cattell and Brennan, 1984). For present purposes we note that the loading weight, b, can henceforth be broken down into a v and an s term. The former says how much the given state is involved in producing a unit change in the dependent variable, the latter how much the state liability itself is modified by the situation before it begins to act on the dependent variable. The s_k's, incidentally, give us a new source of situation descriptions, since each situation can be set out in a vector of values describing how much it affects various state liabilities.

Until more experimentation has been done it is not quite clear whether the s's should be s_{kx} (x being the **particular state** liability) or s_{hkx}, i.e., whether the focal stimulus as well as the ambient situation affects the level of a state. Meanwhile modulation theory seems to apply to many factors that have been considered **traits**, i.e., most traits including intelligence seem to alter slightly with circumstances and need s_k indices. The advantage of modulation theory for practice is that if we need to predict how well individual, i, will do in some future situation, k, we do not need to be there to measure i's states at that moment, but we can infer the levels, knowing i's liability, L_x trait scores and the s_k values for the given situation.

In theory the dynamic calculus recently has gone beyond the split b vs_k, as to a further breakdown of the stimulus situation into p_I, e_I, and s_k. By ordinary analysis of an act we can put down part of the achievement to the subject's **perceptual powers**, p, part to his **motor skills**, which we may call e, for **effectiveness** or execution, and part to the stimulus situation, s_k, which especially acts to modulate the strength of motives. These portions of the discovered b value act on particular kinds of traits. Thus, large p values would be expected on ability traits, notably perceptual abilities, large e loadings would be expected on executive abilities, and large s's on the motivational and state liability factors. We deal with b's, but to be exact, every b could theoretically be broken down by further analysis thus:

$$b = (p + e)s \qquad\qquad (10\text{--}4a)$$

and therefore

$$v = (p + e) \qquad\qquad (10\text{--}4b)$$

The method of breaking down into p, e, and s components is, of course, experimental. To get p we take any differences in execution or situation out of the performance and then factor a set of performances where the differences have to be due purely to perceptual ability differences. To obtain e loadings we wipe out perceptual acts and measure differences purely in execution. For s_k's we have exactly the same performances done in different situations.

Except for the s_k differences no experiment has yet been done in this breakdown so it is premature to ask where it leads. However, we need to be alert to the fact that in the unfolding of behavior from structure, these coefficients are potentially part of further description and prediction.

In laboratory experiments motivation study has always settled down to having subjects accept a certain instruction, we therefore have never taken much note of the unfolding of behavior from one interest to another. This takes place in our daily life as in that of most animals by the impinging of new stimulus situations, one of which has a larger total s_k value than the others, evoking a new set of dynamic (ergic and semic) states. But also in man the internally proceeding thoughts occasion new acts. Reasoning produces new ideas and images, which operate by the s_k values **they** have earned. Indeed, we have not yet sufficiently stressed that the situation, k, is often an entirely internal one. The individual's reaction to a remark on the political situation, for example, may need to be predicted from internal situation, k; namely, that for the last hour he has been boiling internally over the issue.

This recognition of the internal situation brings us to the need for extra terms in the behavioral equation **beyond** the ability, personality, and dynamic unitary traits we have been accustomed to putting there. We need terms for particular internal memories and images, which we will represent by I's thus:

$$a_{hijk} = \Sigma b_{hjkx} A_{xi} + \Sigma b_{hjky} P_{yi} + \Sigma b_{hjkz} D_{zi}$$
$$+ b_{hjkp} I_{pi} + b_{hjkq} I_{qi} \qquad (10\text{--}5)$$

where I_p and I_q are two ideas that have been generated in consciousness at the time. We suppose these are general ideas to everyone, therefore entering into an R-technique analysis. If we thus ascribe action-modifying power to ideas, as images and memories, the critical mind will naturally ask why these have not been found in factor analytic studies before. The answer comes from several directions. First such ideas are very numerous. Second, they would appear only as very small factors. Third, experimenters have not put into experiments the variables necessary to pick them up. Fourth, unlike most major traits they simply are not there most of the time but come and go.

Technically, we can regard specific ideas as **fractions of sems**. If a person happens to be concerned with behavior in which the patriotic sem to country is prominent, then associated ideas will come into mind, such as a dispute about a national boundary recently in the press, which influences what the person shall say presently. The evidence about sems is that they **activate** as a whole but with fragmentary differences in activation of the parts. Probably every sem should be represented as a main M factor with a flock of smaller ideational-emotional factors, I's, around it. These come into action partly through the main modulator, s_k for the sem and partly by modulation, internal and external, specific to themselves. The same is probably true of ergic factors also in which specific forms of behavior have some degree of independence of the main ergic tension. For example, hunger may attach itself to particular foods and the sex erg to particular interest behaviors, needing specific stimuli for their unfolding. Thus, in this chapter we have taken stock of **further** modifications in the behavioral equation in relation to the unfolding of structures into coordinated systems of behavior.

11   The Ego and the Mechanisms of Control

That behavior becomes more adjusted and fitted to a cultural situation by the growth of sems must now be evident, but there remain considerable differences between leaders and normal people, on the one hand, and criminals, alcoholics, neurotics, and psychotics, on the other. In their control despite exposure to the same sentiment growth stimulations, the growth differs among citizens. In this chapter we shall examine the causes of such differences.

In the first place the existence of the second order personality factor Q_{VII} (*UI* 17 in objective tests) loading Q_3, G, and F (-) shows that good home upbringing simultaneously leads to greater development of the superego, G, and the self-sentiment, Q_3, with enhanced *general* inhibition shown by desurgency, F(-). These two controlling sems G and Q_3, share growth of all kinds of normal, social inhibitions and manners, and their levels of development clearly can be seen to control ergs and sems whose expressions are opposed to good behavior.

It is possible, e.g., in most neurotics, to have good ideals associated with poor behavior, and we come here to recognize that ego strength (C factor) must play an important role in control by the very low C factor endowment found in neurotics, alcoholics, and others. A preliminary description of C factor by loadings and and action has been given in Chapter 8, p. 49. It loads positively, **emotionally mature in frustration, stable in interests, calm and unruffled, restrained, and persistent in difficulties**. It is found at highest scores in administrators, airline pilots, and others who face crises of importance daily. It is lowest in all forms of neurosis and psychosis.

The manner in which C factor exercises good control has been described under four headings in Chapter 8. In structural relations C factor has its only marked appearance in a second order factor in Q_{II}, anxiety, where it is about - 0.65. Either low C contributes to a person becoming anxious or high anxiety lowers ego strength. The first is the Freudian hypothesis; the second has much clinical support.

In the common sense of the term C factor is not a sentiment. It lacks any specific attitude-interest content other than an interest in self-control and is clearly different from, for example, the self-sentiment factor, Q_3, which also has interest in self-control as a means to social ends. C is a mechanism of shrewd control of emotional impulses as such. Like any structure it presumably gets learned by success in action. The problem of growth here is that the rewards of restraint are frequently so remote in time and place from the act of restraint that the reinforcement of the act is likely to be very small. Incidentally, if this were not so it should be hard to see why the growth of the ego should not go on indefinitely, giving a much greater relation to age in its time-plot than we actually see. Presumably the growth curve flattens out in middle life because the complication of life is such that no one can make successful rewarding decisions beyond a certain percentage. In a highly predictable environment, where the rewards of control are very steady, we should expect a more continuous increase in the strength of the ego; but as Ecclesiastes says, ... "time and trouble happeneth to them all." Table 11-1 shows some discovered relations to ego strength.

In this connection the large role of the **second** activity of the ego (p. 50) namely, evaluating the probability of consequences in the external world, would lead one to expect a substantial correlation of ego strength with intelligence, but in repeated analyses that correlation has proven to be very low though positive. The possibility must be considered that people make decisions largely in matters at the natural level of their

TABLE 11-1. Known Relations of the Ego Strength Factor, C

Relation of C measures with ratings and behavior records

Positively with:	Emotional stability
	Maturity
	Readiness to face realities
	(with GZ scales of activity, ascendance, objectivity and "masculinity")
Negatively with:	Unstable
	Easily annoyed
	Dissatisfied with life
	Sleep disturbances, etc.

intelligence, so that the more intelligent also face more risks—or at least the same risks—of failure.

The role of what we suspect to be the most determined influence genetically—the role in Step 3 of calling halt to all impulse while a reasoned decision is made—is central in impulse deflection, and we might expect, therefore, the substantial (about 0.5) heritability we find in C measures (Cattell, 1981). Process number 1, internally sizing up the strengths of various needs, might also have a hereditary component.

We are left to consider the fourth and last process in C, namely, effect implementation of a decision by CET invocation of dynamic structures that help defend and maintain the decision. This requires that the person be well aware of his collection of dynamic traits and possess imagination in seeing which will align themselves as allies to enforce the decision reached. We suspect that this procedure would be much subject to training and experience. The smoker seeking to give up the habit needs to be able to call up all his sems and ergs which are opposed to smoking each time he has an impulse to smoke, such as a sports sem, the self-sentiment regarding health, etc. The more powerful ego knows more of such potential allies and has the CET skills to call them into action. As various teaching centers realize, this CET is an ego skill open to improvement by practice. In practice Heather Cattell (1984) reports quite a number of increases in ego strength brought about by attention to the four parts of its action. An interesting case is the finding by Cattell et al. (1966) of a steady improvement of C score simply through the therapeutic use of a sedative drug (Miltown) over a short period, as shown in Figure 11–1. This change in six weeks is significant and may be due to such sedative reduction of general emotionality of reactions as convinced the individuals of gain in control.

In studying the ego and its growth we need to take account of what psychoanalysis has called defense mechanisms. Cattell and Wenig (1952) investigated the factorial existence of such unitary mechanisms and were able to verify several and their relation to personality factors in perceptual activities. For example, true projection factors out as a unitary tendency, distinct from naive projection as positively correlated with L factor (protension), while fantasy is related to factor, O, guilt proneness (0.45). Psychoanalytically the defense mechanisms are regarded as substitutes for true, realistic ego action, dragged in as immediate defenses in stressful, traumatic circumstances. Thus, in projection defense "I hate him" becomes "He hates me" which, not involving internal readjustments, is easier to handle. Similarly, fantasy

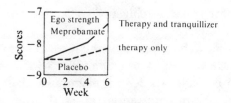

	Change in drug therapy group (1)	t value (2)	Change in placebo-therapy group (3)	t value (4)	Differ-ence (1) and (3)	t value
Ego strength	1.24	2.88 $p > .005$	.48	.83 (n.s.)	.76	1.11 (n.s.)
Guilt-proneness	.52	1.21 (n.s.)	1.05	2.69 $p > .01$	−.53	.97 (n.s.)

FIGURE 11-1. Effect of psychotherapy on ego strength, C, with reduction of emotional upsets.

gives a degree of satisfaction that saves the ego the task of coming to terms with reality, especially where the problem is that real satisfaction would produce guilt and unworthiness, O factor. The ego itself would curb such desires by revealing their incompatibility with external reality and other dynamic traits within the person. Indeed, realistic has one of the highest ratings among traits loaded by the ego factor, and this calls on us to recognize that acceptance of reality is central in ego action, as represented in processes number 1 and 2.

In the interaction of the ego with the satisfaction of the sems we need to examine the roles of the general states: anxiety, depression, guilt, regression, stress, arousal, and fatigue. These are distinct from the state levels on specific ergs, though like the latter they have frequently been classed as motivation states, e.g., by Spence and Taylor (1951) and others.

The genesis of the general states is seen most clearly in the APA chart (p. 44) where arousal as the summation of all ergic arousal can turn to anger under frustration, then to anxiety and to depression, regression, and neurotic reactions if frustration persists. We can regard anxiety as a state of deposit of ergic tensions while there is still hope of their satisfaction. It shows itself centrally in a disturbance of the autonomic system with higher pulse and blood pressure, greater ketosteroid excretion, and other physiological measures tested by Cattell and Scheier (1961, p. 198). Since this anxiety can be reduced and reissued in motivational action of specific kinds, it is correct to speak of it as a general potential motivation, striving for drive reduction.

The level of anxiety in a given individual and circumstance has been formulated (Spielberger, 1972) as due to three circumstances:

1. situational uncertainty in regard to fear of deprivation
2. inherent fear of loss of control by the ego
3. anxiety from sheer and certain deprivation.

The first appears in most life situations in which great uncertainty about satisfaction exists. It can be formulated as

$$a_{ei} = (f)(E_{xi} + M_{yi}E_{xi})V_d \, (E_{fi} - H_i) \qquad (11\text{-}1)$$

where E_x is the erg under doubt, present in its own strength and in the semic bond; V_d is the degree of uncertainty of satisfaction; E_f is the endowment in the fear erg; and H is the parmia personality factor showing small response to fear.

The second anxiety component can be formulated as

$$a_{ci} = (f) \, \frac{(E_{xi} + M_{yi}E_{xi})}{(C + Q_3) - v(E_{xi} + M_{yi}E_{xi})} \qquad (11\text{-}2)$$

Here C and Q_3 represent the strength of ego and the self-sem, v is a scaling weight, and the remainder are the strength of the need. This implies that if $v\,(E_{xi} + M_{yi}E_{xi})$ is large, the natural controls $(C + Q_3)$ are threatened and anxiety increases proportionally.

The last component in anxiety is simply the strength of the frustrated erg thus:

$$a_{pi} = (f)(E_{xi} + M_{yi}E_{xi}) - E_{xri} \qquad (11\text{-}3)$$

where the first term is the desired satisfaction and E_{xri} is what may really take place. Then the total anxiety, A_{xi} is given by

$$A_{xi} = a_{ei} + a_{ci} + a_{pi} \qquad (11\text{-}4)$$

Anxiety is thus in the main a garbage pail into which three sources of production are poured. All three contain references to inherent traits of the subject; those such as C, H, and Q_3 show their role by entering into the second order anxiety factor.

Depression comes later in the APA process where hope of expression disappears. It has a more positive function than has commonly been supposed because it occurs in major setbacks and discourages all action along the lines then being pursued. Its function would seem to be to dissolve existing dynamic trends and throw the individual back to the emergence of radically different dynamic systems. Perhaps we see this most clearly in the suffering and renunciations of saintly types such as Loyola or St. Catherine, who finally say they are reborn. In any case, it is frequently a sign that the things sought are the wrong ones, though they may spring even from an overactive superego.

The state of regression was first treated as a seeming treat in factoring of objective personality tests in 1945–46 independently by Cattell (1946) and Eysenck (1947). It loads such behaviors as low ratio of accuracy to speed, greater rigidity, greater momentary oscillation of performance, higher suggestibility, and poorer memory. The individual is aware of his attitudes, and has skills, but seems unable to hang on to them and to mobilize himself. It has now repeatedly been found unduly high in neurotics; (Eysenck called it "neuroticism," but neurotics differ even more on other factors, and psychotics also appear very low (Cattell, Schmidt, & Bjerstedt, 1972) on this factor. The label regression is meant to imply that dynamics in the Freudian sense has been withdrawn from once more advanced uses. It is correlated in the expected direction with weak ego and seems to represent a partial contribution to dislocation of ego functions.

The remaining general states need comment only for *stress*, which was not recognized as a totally different state from anxiety before extensive P-technique factoring. It *does* overlap on some physiological measures (Cattell & Scheier, 1961) such as heightened blood pressure and ketosteroid excretion but is otherwise very different. Effort stress, as it can best be called, occurs in physical and mental effort without anxiety or other pathology. For example, it is found in somatic neurotics, who tackle a problem vigorously rather than in ordinary neurotics who retreat from a problem with anxiety and guilt. The eight or more general states thus have close relations to dynamic adjustments, and to the role of the ego in controlling them.

12   The Laws and Equations
of Structured Learning

Having looked over the domain of the dynamic calculus from the nature of the dynamic structures through the equations of their conflicts, interactions, and control, we are ready to study the learning process in a more systematic fashion.

Whereas reflexology (behaviorism) considers two processes which Skinner has labelled *CR I* (Pavlovian conditioning) and *CR II* (learning with reward), the new structural learning considers **five** which we will first describe.

1. **Co-Excitation.** Here two stimuli or responses that occur simultaneously come to be associated in that the future stimulation by one tends to reinstate the other. This is the old law of association expressed afresh in Pavlovian conditioning. It supposes that an **engram**, a change in neural connections such that one idea or stimulus invokes a particular second idea, is formed by a connection when one center of excitation in the brain runs across to another center simultaneously created.

The coming together of the two experiences may occur:

   a. Through two external stimuli, as in Pavlovian classical conditioning;

   b. By what Spearman (1923) called a noegenetic act of education, as when one asks what is the opposite of contracting a debt, thereby, asociating gift and debt. All kinds of reasoning employ relationships constantly and bring ideas together by association;

65

c. By an act of retrieval, bringing a new idea into consciousness at the same time as an idea being entertained. This may occur through an emotional state, which we know tends to excite the retrieval of some ideas more than others.

Co-excitation is sometimes called contiguity learning, but it involves more than contiguity. The CE law, as we may label co-excitation effects, involves **fusion** as well as contiguousness. The fusion may run more in one direction than the other, notably from the earlier to the secondary stimulus and from the lesser to the greater excitation. It is easy to see that in a long life practically every stimulus would become associated with every other, producing a random chaos in retrieval (Estes et al., 1957). All experiments agree, however, in assigning very little accruing strength to the engram from a single co-occurence, and it is only by certain statistically greater frequencies that we get appropriate retrievals (Konorski, 1948; Egger & Miller, 1963; Mackintosh, 1974). A dictatorship of the recent and accidental in memory would make logical and purposeful behavior impossible. Perhaps what happens in schizophrenics in the absence of strong purposes produces the puns and bizarre logic of their associations.

2. **Means-End (ME) Learning or CR II.** What has been called operant conditioning, CR II—to try to bring it into the classical conditioning paradigm of Pavlov—is actually a very different thing from classical conditioning. In its constant essence it is learning a new piece of behavior because it brings one more readily to the semic or ergic goal. The role of reward and deprivation (punishment) in shaping behavior has been realized since the dawn of history, but the many experiments by reflexologists have brought in certain laws mainly established with animals. What they note are:

a. The more rewarded responses, by quicker consummatory satisfaction of an erg, are reinstated more frequently on future occasions.

b. The higher the drive strength, the more rapid the learning, except at very high drive.

c. The closer the reward to a given stimulus response, the more rapid the learning. The responses in animals are mainly blind trial-and-error responses so that superstitious behavior, which does not really advance to the goal, can temporarily get memory value.

d. There are few natural learning situations in which co-excitation (CE) and means-end learning (ME) do not in fact interact. As Blodgett (1929) showed long ago, exposure to a maze at almost unrewarded levels of motivation leads to better performance when subsequently rewarded than appears in less rewarded controls. The evidence is discussed by Meehl and MacCorquodale (1948), Rescorla and Solomon (1967), and others working on sensory preconditioning, latent learning, and Tolman's cognitive maps, showing that association has often done its work before any decisive means-end motivation enters.

e. There are some findings on drive shift and reward shift. The latter shows that a group learning under lower reward and performing less well will catch up with a well-rewarded group in two or three equally well-rewarded runs. This again supports the importance of sheer cognitive association learning.

f. In drive shift we find that after learning something under one drive, there is marked loss of performance when shifted to another drive. This fits our use of the dynamic lattice.

g. The phenomena of extinction of behavior with unrewarded practice, habituation, and reminiscence in their reflexological meanings introduce new aspects to means-end learning.

h. There are now well-checked laws on the effects of frequency of trials, spacing, temporal regularity and irregularity of reward, and all the formulations possible among the **peripheral**, outside entities with which a strictly reflexological approach alone deals.

Before going beyond CR I and CR II we should note that CR I, as distinct from CE, is not as much a **principle** as a prescribed experimental **paradigm**. If we suppose that a spinal reflex belongs to the class of a **motive** (to sneeze or blink the eye is a relief), then CR I becomes means-end learning in which the new stimulus for the behavior is artificially introduced instead of occurring by chance as in operant conditioning. The conditioned stimulus becomes a means to the goal of the reflex release. At the same time the closeness of the new and the natural stimulus adds a co-excitation effect to the new stimulus. Thus,

CR *I* is not purely a new principle from CR *II* but an artificially arranged admixture of *CE* and *ME* effects.

3. **Integration Learning, N.** A very important form of learning in clinical psychology but scarcely recognized in animal, reflexological research must now be added among the three extra principles to CR *I* and CR *II* in structured learning. It appears in the behavior where a new course of action is found which achieves the objective of two or more existing courses. Normally it will do so with some individual conflict still remaining (p.IPR) but with an overall gain in satisfaction. This learning can occur with insight or by trial-and-error experiment.

N learning is in effect an *ME* or *CE* learning, but it involves something new that probably leads to special laws. Principally it involves inhibition of one behavior or both before the new solution and therefore usually involves action of the ego.

4. **Ergic Goal Modification (GM Learning).** The phenomenon in which not only the path to the ergic goal but the ergic goal **itself** is modified was first studied in clinical psychology by Freud as **sublimation**. It cannot occur without death in self-preserving ergs, but it can in the more flexible race-preserving ergs such as sex and parental-pitying behavior. Here, for example, "a full stomach may be a remedy for an empty heart," and various deviations occur, partly culturally useful, partly perversions. Experimental evidence for change of actual consummatory goal has been hard to come by except perhaps in the work of Hess (1958), Forgus (1955), and Muktananda (1974).

5. **Energy-Saving or Rest-Seeking Erg.** There are countless evidences of the gradual dropping of unnecessary steps in learned courses of action, beginning with Meehl and MacCorquodale's (1948) experiment on elimination of blind maze entrances. Whether this saving of effort is an extra principle in all learning or to be explained simply by the presence of the rest-seeking erg is, however, still uncertain. If the latter, such learning would occur more rapidly in tired animals. Certainly most humans find themselves unconsciously dropping some necessary step in a learned chain from time to time, and there are many broad cultural instances, e.g., the dropping of gender and inflection in speech by the Anglo-Saxons.

The description of change in learning has to be criticized in existing treatments not only for

  a. restricting to two principles but also
  b. omitting allowance over the time of learning for genetic, maturational changes

c. recording change in the dependent variable but not in the traits and indices that describe how the new behavior is brought about.

Regarding the second charge which becomes important, for example, in changes in school children taken over a year or more, we will simply say that a principle and formula has been worked out elsewhere in behavior genetics (Cattell, 1981) to show the relation of the **environmentally produced part** of a trait change to specific features of the environment that may be affecting it thus:

$$r_{e_x t_y} = \frac{r_{e_x}(g+t)y}{r_{t_y}(g+t)y} \tag{12-1}$$

Here $r_{e_x t_y}$ gives the regression of the environmental part of trait, y, namely t_y on the environmental change in the environmentally determined feature, x. The numerator in (12–1), the correlation of trait e_x with the total variance, $(g+t)$, is obtained from the PLA experiment (p.IPR) and the denominator from knowing the heritability of trait x, in regard to which H value we have:

$$r^2_{t_y}(g+t)y = 1 - H \tag{12-2}$$

There is a second way of reaching this environmentally susceptible part of trait y and to find its relation to the various environmental features, x, z, etc., given in the same Chapter 6 of Cattell, 1981. Granted that we are dealing with measures of trait y from which maturation effects have been excluded, the full task before us is to find by correlation or factor analysis the change between a pre- and postoperation measure of all traits, A, P, and D, of all behavioral indices for these traits. It has been pointed out that through separate, controlled experiments we can split the behavioral indices, b's, into three terms: p, a perceptual involvement; e, an effectiveness of execution term; and s_k, a modulation index which states how much the liability to the given state or trait is modulated by the given situation, k. According to the mode of calculation, b can equal the sum or the product of the three, but psychologically we prefer

$$b = vs_k = (p + e)s_k \tag{12-3}$$

Part (a)   Specification Equation for a Single Performance (Prior to Learning Change)
Expressed in Matrix Form

$$a_{hijk} = I' \, D_p \, D_r \, D_i \, D_s \, D_t \, I \tag{3-4}$$

As matrix diagrams:

Part (b)   Change from Prelearning to Postlearning Performance,

$$a_{hijk}(2) - a_{hijk}(1) = a_{hijk}(l)$$

(Where l = Learning Increment) in Matrix Form

$$a_{hijk}(l) = I' \, D_{p2} \, D_{r2} \, D_{i2} \, D_{s2} \, D_{t2} \, I - I' \, D_{p1} \, D_{r1} \, D_{i1} \, D_{s1} \, D_{t1} \, I \tag{3-5a}$$

or, as a percentage change,

$$a_{hijk}(l) = \frac{I' \, D_{p2} \, D_{r2} \, D_{i2} \, D_{s2} \, D_{t2} \, I}{I' \, (D_{p1} \, D_{r1} \, D_{s1} \, D_{t1}) \, I} \times 100 \tag{3-5b}$$

Note these are restatements of equations (3-3a) and (3-3b) in matrix form. D_p is a diagonal matrix of the y values for the y factors concerned, and similarly for the proficiency and interest coefficients in D_r and D_i, the modulator values in D_s, and the trait values in D_t. The identity matrix I and its transpose I' are there only as part of the matrix mechanics, to collect the terms from the diagonal multiplications—$p_a r_a i_a s_a T_a + p_b r_b i_b s_b T_b + \ldots$, and so forth ($a$ and b being two traits)—into a single scalar, a_{hijk}.

Part (c)

Behavior Change:	$a_{hijk}(2\text{-}1)$
Perception Index Change:	$p(2) - p(1)$
Motor Proficiency Index Change:	$r(2) - r(1)$
Interest-Motivation Index Change:	$i(2) - i(1)$
Modulation Index Change:	$s(2) - s(1)$
Trait Change:	$T(2) - T(1)$

Descriptively, for various psychological analytic purposes, we can dissect the behavior change into changes in five vectors, of which one term in each is illustrated above. However, we cannot *predict or calculate* $a_{hijk}(2\text{-}1)$ from these differences of vectors (not knowing the original vectors), since in general the difference of two (or more) products cannot be resolved into the product of the differences of the elements.

FIGURE 12-1. Comprehensive statement of structured learning change as a five-vector outcome.

This permits the role of the trait in its actual involvement, v, in producing the behavioral variable to be determined by two experiments, giving additively a p and an e, while the s_k is separately determined as described in Figure 12–1.

In their change between the two occasions the p and the e describe the change in the mode of use of the subjects' perceptual and executive skills, respectively. The change in s_k describes the change in motivation-interest in probable terms mainly of new weight on the dynamic structure factors. The vector of s_k changes and defines the changes to the extent to which the situation evokes the interests of the various dynamic traits as a result of the learning experience.

This should be an extremely valuable vector in all kinds of emotional learning research for it tells us what new dynamic traits enter into the motivation. For example, when boy meets girl it may happen as part of the learning that the b value in the attitude "I want to see X again" will go up on the sex and parental protective ergs. In general, the **totality** of learning change in a given attitude is represented by four vectors, thus:

$$(p_{2x} - p_{1x}), (p_{2y} - p_{1y})(p_{2z} - p_{1z}), \text{etc.}$$
$$(e_{2x} - e_{1x}), (e_{2y} - e_{1y})(e_{2z} - e_{1z}), \text{etc.}$$
$$(s_{2kx} - s_{1kx}), (s_{2ky} - s_{1ky})(s_{2kz} - s_{1kz}), \text{etc.}$$
$$(T_{2xi} - T_{1xi}), (T_{2yi} - T_{1yi})(T_{2zi} - T_{1zi}), \text{etc.} \qquad (12\text{–}4)$$

though we may be content with running the p and e vectors into a single, nonmotivational v vector.

The manner of **simultaneously** calculating the changes on the behavioral indices and the T's, the traits, is set out elsewhere (Cattell, 1980, p. 203). If we use the p and e in a product relation and take the pre- and postrelations as a series of quotients, p_2/p_1, e_2/e_1, s_{k_2}/s_{k_1}, and T_2/T_1, then the change from a_{hijk_1} to a_{hijk_2} can be expressed in matrix terms by diagonal matrices of the quotients, as shown in Figure 12–1.

By R-technique the behavioral indices in the above equation normally will be average values for the groups, but by P-technique we can find those specific to the learning of a given individual. It will be seen that in structured learning we have a far more analytical and comprehensive statement of learning than occurs in conditioning statements of total change in a variable. We find both changes in the total vector of traits (since learning rarely affects but one) and in the vectors of **application** of the traits. There still remains the task of relating this fuller picture to the action of the fuller list of learning principles in the first part of this chapter and we shall approach this in the following chapters.

13   The Role of Personality and Learning Laws in Human Learning

In the preceding chapter we have considered the change of a specific behavior by learning as resoluble into changes on a number of broad, common factors. It **may** happen that the change is largely on a specific factor, but in personality our interest will always lie in the broad factors. Probably the change in T will occur more in the ability, A, and the dynamic, D, factors than in more heritable personality-temperament, P, factors.

If the learning experiment concentrates on a particular skill or attitude, the change on others may be small. What we are witnessing in that case is that a sem, D_x, increases in score by a change in just one of the attitudes it loads or by the addition to it of an attitude it did not load before. This opens up to us an observation on the way sems grow. **They increase in their areas of reference by gaining some degree of satisfaction from each new attitude.** For example, a sentiment to one's dog may add an attitude of approval to some commercial dog food that the dog shows he likes. It may also develop regarding the licensing laws for dogs. Henceforth the activation of the dog sem is also likely to bring these attendant attitudes near to consciousness as part of the total engram action. Such addenda may show relatively low loading on the broad common sem pattern because only a few people include these subsidiary attitudes.

The initial acquisition of sems and ability factors probably arises through operation of the ME law by which the sem **object** has offered a way to an ergic goal. Perhaps in the case of the dog the satisfaction of the parental-protective erg occurred when the owner saw him as a sad, lonely puppy. Thereafter the CE law can play an increasing part as ideas and events attach themselves to the dog. For example, there were the times when the dog warned of a burglar or bit a neighbor's cat, both adding to the meaning of the sem. The remaining three learning principles also may have extended the meaning of the sem and the ergic investment in it.

We have known from ancient times that the growth of a new sem tends to remove some motivation from earlier ones. (This often causes jealousy when the competing objects are people.) On the other hand, if new sems subsidiate to earlier ones, this scarcely happens. Thus, if a researcher acquires a sem for a foreign language that serves research interests, there is little loss; but if the researcher gets interested in chorus girls, the shift of ergic satisfactions may bite into career interests. Any calculation of shift in ergic investment in sems therefore has to take the subsidiations in the dynamic lattice into account. If the two competing sems are not subsidiated, the growth of satisfactions of ergs in one (other things being equal) is going to cause a corresponding drop in the ergic investment pattern in the other. A satisfied husband is a poor prospect for a hunting female. It would seem, however, that in understanding learning some expression for the **resistance** in established semic systems need to be introduced.

Meanwhile, let us consider the operation of ME learning in basic situations epitomized by maze learning as studied in animals. Here we have the common situation with much human learning that there is trial-and-error, operant conditioning on the way to reward at some ultimate goal. First, we face the problem of considering reward as a fall of ergic tension (the drive reduction theory of reward). The assumption begins with the notion that because ergic tension causes goal-striving its elimination by consummatory satisfaction will bring striving to an end and be the reward.

The problem in this statement is that in a maze, for example, there is much evidence that the ergic tension **increases** from the goal approach signs as the animal approaches the food at the goal box. This requires that the animal actually seek higher tension levels though they are regarded as unpleasant and averse. Let us consider in Figure 13–1 an animal rerunning a maze to which it has some familiarity. It will recognize by certain subgoals that it is approaching the food. We know from human experience that it will get more excited and motivated as it approaches its goal. We can imagine either an increase in motivation as each subgoal is reached or a decrease because a subgoal has been attained, giving us curves as in Figure 12–1 (a) or (b). In either case, however, we have to admit that excitation and arousal *rise* from beginning to end, presenting us with the concept that since drive reduction is reward, the process cannot be rewarding as it proceeds.

An escape from this predicament is to recognize that arousal (ergic tension) and need strength are not the same thing—as already recognized in Equation (6–1)—and that reward is reduction in *need* strength. Over

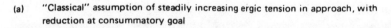

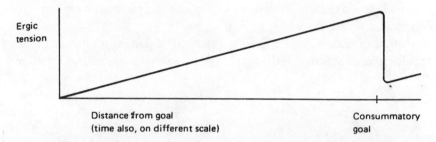

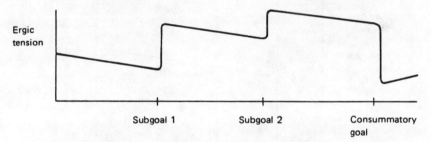

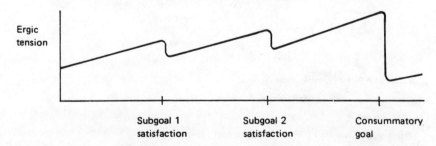

FIGURE 13–1. Some earlier alternative hypotheses regarding tension change in approach to goal through subgoal appeals.

the course of the maze run need strength will remain unchanged except for the slight increase in appetite with time which would occur regardless of the animal being in or out of the maze. Its slight rise offers no aversion to the maze run, but the arousal will mount with each new stimulating subgoal met in the maze as shown in Figure 13-2.

For brevity let us write ergic need strength in Equation 6-1 simply as E and ergic tension as E. We will then state as a learning law that the engram amount achieved is a product of the *arousal* strength and the strength of the cognitive experience. In this way we can account for the well-known fact that new, successful behaviors nearer the goal are more rapidly learned than more remote behaviors and various other learning observations (Figure 13-3).

We can reasonably suppose that any cognitive experience, e.g., the recollection of the turn of the maze that the animal took, will reverberate

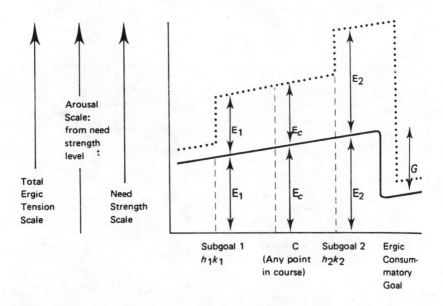

Key

_____ = Need strength curve: Plot of E

.... = Arousal strength curve: Plot of E

Ergic tension = E = E + E

G = Reward (gratification) by fall of need strength tension at goal, G

FIGURE 13-2. Hypothesis of course of need strength and arousal on way to consummatory behavior.

with diminishing intensity after it has occurred—in Figure 13-3 we suppose the decline with time is linear. At the time the animal reaches this goal the reverberatory remnant will be less for the more remote acts. If we let E_R represent the reduction of need on arousal that occurs as the goal reward, then our hypothesis in Figure 13-3 is that

$$\eta = a_{j2} - a_{ji} = E_R \cdot m/t \qquad (13\text{-}1)$$

where η is engram amount, m is the strength of the cognitive experience at the time of the operant response—which we suppose helps toward the goal—and t is a function of the time lapse between it and the reward.

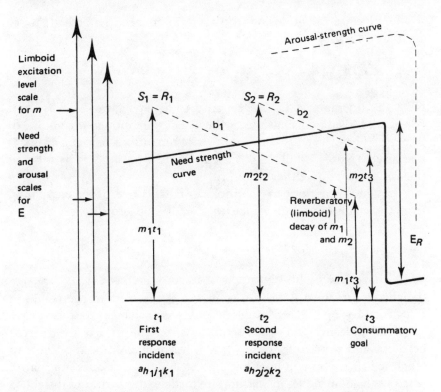

Note $hk = S$, and $j = R$, in stimulus-response notation. m_1t_1 and m_2t_2 are the proto-engram activities immediately at the time of response, and m_1t_2' and m_2t_3 at time t_3 of the reward, E_R. The extent of final engramming (first response) is hypothesized to be the product $E_R m_1 t_3$.

FIGURE 13-3. Engramming hypothesized as a product of cognitive reverberatory trace and need reduction as a goal.

Alternatively we may find that better results are achieved by taking the fall in the *need* strength as the reward, E_1.

If we are to include the full action of human learning, we must consider the weights also on ability and other personality factors that we know determine learning. The prediction of school achievement, for example, can go up to 75 percent of the variance on the achievement variable from A, P, and D source traits alone with nothing said about reward or other learning principles (Cattell & Butcher, 1967). Consequently, if we consider both traits and reward we reach an initial equation for a new engram, η.

$$\eta = \Sigma v_a s_a A + \Sigma v_p s_p p + \Sigma v_d s_d D + E_R m/t \qquad (13\text{-}2)$$

With certain assumptions the last term can be expanded into more detail as follows:

$$E_R m/t + N \cdot E_r (vs_{ke} E + vs_{km} ME + vs_{km} M)/t \qquad (13\text{-}3)$$

Here the operant act R_2 in response to S_k in Figure 13-3 is itself considered fixed in magnitude by the usual expression in the middle of Equation (13-3), and N is the number of repetitions before learning is measured. (Note Cattell (1980) used $-t$ instead of dividing by y, but at present speculation either would fit.)

It is important not to overlook the **difference** of the engram, η, from the change in performance, $(a_{j2} - a_{j1})$. The latter is

$$(a_{j2i} - a_{j1i}) = \Sigma (b_{j2} - b_{j1})(T_{2i} - T_{1i}) + b_{j2n} \eta_i \qquad (13\text{-}4)$$

i.e., we have to work back from the observed increment in $(a_{j2i} - a_{j1i})$ to the changes in the b's and the value $b_{j2n} \eta_i$ and then to the values in Equation (13-2) where the other predictions of change take their place.

It might seem that the above equations, deriving from trial-and-error behavior and restricting to CR II, ME learning, are not applicable to much insightful human learning. In fact, however, it does not matter whether the new moves in learning are made with or without insight so far as their reward is concerned. Every insight is a **tentative** insight and its sure reward does not occur until the goal is reached; it may, however, show a slower reverberating extinction than a blind act.

What distinguishes most human learning is *mental* experimentation in place of actual experimentation and the greater role of CE learning based on reasoning. For example, farmer George wants to learn if he should buy more cows. He finds (CE) that his neighbor does well with three acres of grazing to a cow and since he personally has 60 acres, a brief calculation leads to his buying eight more. All this is done in terms of imagery and the vast supply of symbols which humans learn to use, but the same five laws of learning hold as with a concretely worked-out piece of animal learning.

14 Social and Perceptual Settings: The Econetic Model

So far we have attended to the environment to the extent of showing that its effect on any act can be expressed in three vectors: p, e, and s. This can be extended, however, to a depiction of the total social environment in which people live and act the **econetic model**.

First sallies into the contribution of the environment began with such research as that of Endler and Hunt (1969), and Magnusson (1976) on the fractions of variance in anxiety responses that belonged to (1) person differences and (2) environment-response differences. We see advances also in the differentiations of role behaviors from personality behaviors and in the perceptual problems of spectrad (attribution) theory, all of which we must cover here.

However, from the standpoint of complete statistical, quantitative coverage we do best to step over these partial approaches and go to the Basic Data Relation Matrix (*BDRM*) once called the covariation chart (Cattell, 1946). This goes down to **the fact that any psychological event has five signatures**: a given person acting, i; a given stimulus, h; a given act (response), j; a given ambient situation, s; and a given observer, o.

A particular response measurement, a_{hijko}, resides in a cell of a five-dimensional score matrix, shown for three visible dimensions in Figure 14–1, which we may call a data box (*BDRM*), since it contains **all** the basic data that psychology can use.

The variance of the data in the box can be broken down initially in five ways: by people, by types of response, by stimuli, by situations, and by observers. Endler and Hunt (1969) did so, for example, comparing people and situations in anxiety responses.

However, if we take covariance into account we can take correlations over various faces of the box finding factors and weights for each. These

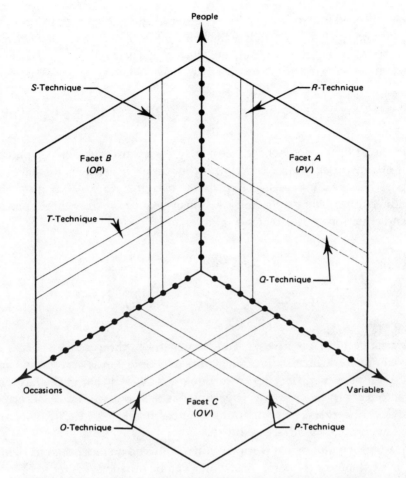

Only three of the five dimensions can be shown pictorially here. The missing coordinates are "observers" and "stimuli" (When variables are split into responses and stimuli).

FIGURE 14-1. The basic data relation matrix (BDRM) with three kinds of ids. Only three of the five dimensions can be shown pictorially here. The missing coordinates are "observers" and "stimuli" (when variables are split into responses and stimuli).

procedures constitute what have been called R-technique (face of people by tests others averaged); P-technique, (face of occasions (situations) by tests); Q-technique (face of tests by people); etc. through $20 = 2^5 C_2$ possibilities when we include transpose faces as in Q-technique. (See Figure 14–1 for these correlations.)

The covariance approach, seeking factors behind the variables, can be followed in two ways: person-centered and additive. In the person-centered approach we analyze the behavior of people in terms of factors in tests, situations, stimuli, etc. and add them all into a behavior equation with four dimensions:

$$a_{hijko} = \Sigma b_{jx} T_{xi} + \Sigma b_{by} T_{yi} + \Sigma b_{kz} T_{zi} + \Sigma b_{op} T_{pi} \quad (14\text{-}1)$$

In the additive approach we factor all terms against each other. Omitting the transposes which contribute the same covariance, we have ten possible combinations of five things two at a time. With just three dimensions: over i's, j's, and k's, however, we have only three analyses and equations (all R-technique):

$$a_{ij} = b_{j1} T_{1i} + \ldots + b_{jn} T_{ni}$$
$$a_{jk} = w_{k1} P_{1j} + \ldots + w_{km} P_{mj}$$
$$a_{ik} = y_{i1} Q_{1k} + \ldots + y_{ip} Q_{pk} \quad (14\text{-}2)$$

Variance in a_{hij} is now an addition of these three score sources of covariance, estimated through factors in people, kinds of response, and situations. The difference from Equation 14-1 is that in the latter all factors are **in the person**, governing his relations to stimuli, response styles, observers, and situations whereas in Figure 14-2 they spring from completely different sources.

An account of motivation requires us to do no more than recognize the existence of these models, which can be pursued further in **N-way factor analysis** elsewhere (Cattell, Blaine, & Brennan, 1984). The person-centered model (14-1) is most relevant to motivation and environment for in a motivational act it tells us what factors contribute from the nature of the person and the person's responses to stimulus conditions, situational conditions, etc.

A still broader approach recognizes the differences in cultural backgrounds. The syntality of a culture can be recognized and defined in a **syntality profile** for the culture on dimensions common to all national cultures; however, the cultural elements for personality motivation use probably can be represented better in terms of the strength of various elements: schools, police, libraries, recreational opportunities, etc. This can be done by numbers in a **cultural syntality** matrix which for further use has to be diagonal as in Figure 14-2.

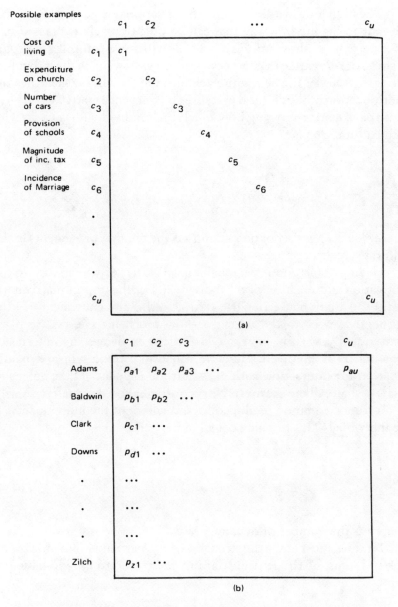

Illustration of the cultural syntality and personal position matrices C and P.
(a) Cultural syntality matrix: C; (b) personal position or relative matrix: P.

FIGURE 14-2. The cultural syntality and personal relevance matrices for econstic studies.

The individual within a culture finds various elements more or less relevant to his life in a way that can be quantitatively expressed in a separate matrix, shown in Figure 14-2, which we can call a personal position or **relevance** matrix because it shows how much the individual needs to concern himself with each element. It will be seen that the multiplication of the cultural pressure and relevance matrices will yield an **impact** matrix showing how much each individual has to do with each cultural element.

$$P \quad \times \quad C \quad = \quad I$$
$$(N \times u) \quad (u \times u) \quad (N \times u) \qquad (14\text{-}3)$$

where N is the number of people and u is the number of elements in the cultural syntality.

Having obtained the personal impact matrix, I, we can turn to the motivational interaction of the individual. For the impact matrix itself is still in situational, ecometric terms, stating the equivalent of how frequently i goes to the movie or how much income tax he pays. Consequently, we now have to consider the exchanges in I in terms of dynamic traits involved. Here we can utilize the b's in a dynamic equation for interaction with each cultural element. These values in what we shall call the **ecometric-psychological bridge** matrix, E, will, of course, be common to all people and will omit the individuality of the individual. This bridging equation becomes:

$$I \quad \times \quad E \quad = \quad G$$
$$(N \times u) \quad (u \times z) \quad (N \times z) \qquad (14\text{-}4)$$

where z is the number of dynamic traits.

Next we must enter the strengths of the particular dynamic traits, ergs and sems, **of the individual** in a matrix, D, to individualize the result:

$$G \quad \cdot \quad D \quad = \quad Q$$
$$(N \times z) \quad (N \times z) \quad (N \times z) \qquad (14\text{-}5)$$

Here the dot between G and D indicates that the multiplication rule is different from the ordinary one. It requires that each cell in G be multiplied by the corresponding cell in D which gives each trait's involvement, giving in Q the involvement for each individual of each of the z dynamic traits. This is a statement of the individual's total dynamic involvement in culture.

If we put the separate steps together, we now have what may be called the general cultural environment equation for the individual thus:

$$(P \times C \times E) \cdot D = Q \qquad (14\text{-}6)$$

In putting this together we get $P \times S$ by inspection of the culture. E is the important unknown, D and G come from a dynamic factor analysis, and Q is a measurable end result. The value of E for social psychology is immense; it represents the dynamic investment typical for numerous cultural entities. It will be noticed that the above matrices can be handled in alternative orders. For example, E could come earlier, putting the dynamic analysis before the impact matrix, but the above seems more practicable.

In the social area there remains to discuss the treatment of roles. A role will appear among personality factors, given role behavior data in the factoring. It is recognizable by spreading its loadings over most personality factor loadings and by being peculiar to special situations. In its marked response to s_k's in particular situations, it is reminiscent of a state. Ultimately, it is to be checked by the individual's awareness, in general, that these loaded behaviors occur only when adopting a role.

A final dynamic model in the social area is that in determining attribution, the assignment of motives to others and the degree of inaccuracy in that assignment. Here we go to the **spectrad** model (Cattell, 1982c) which in turn factors many judges, judging the traits of one person and many subjects rated by a single (main) judge. The former yields the relation between misperceptions of the observed and the **traits of the observers**, which we call the **construing** equation. The second experimental situation yields relations between other traits in **the observed person** and misperceptions in the trait set to be rated which we call the **contextual** equation. Similar, parallel analyses can be made with **groups** as to the misperception of the b's rather than the traits. This tells us how the general motivation on a course of action gets misperceived in each situation. This whole spectrad theory treatment hinges on **perception** being defined by the behavioral equation as what one would **do** with the exposed object, i.e., the behavioral equation contains the **meaning** of the object or course of action seen. The meaning can be broken down by the p, e, and s indices into three aspects of meaning, the motivational, i, and the s's being the most important vector here. Meanwhile equation 14–06 remains one of the most central models in socio-cultural psychology.

15 Some Reflections on the Action of Control Traits

With the above view over the whole personality-situation field to draw upon, let us return to the problem of integration of all behavior on the personality which we began to study in Chapter 11 on the ego and the mechanisms of control. The general personality theory propounded here has been called the *VIDA* model (**vector-id description**) (Cattell 1980) because it analyzes structure into **ids**, i.e., factorial traits behind behavior (as in the data box, Chapter 9) acting in **vectors**, i.e., combining their effects with special weights. This vector-id analysis requires final reality to be put into a **systems theory** of interaction, which we shall attempt in the next chapter on the *VIDAS* theory; but for the present we shall proceed to the summit of the *VIDA* model in its depiction of control and integration.

From their behavioral content and role in prediction of criteria, we have recognized three factors formally concerned with control: the ego (C), the superego (G), and the self-sentiment (Q_3). However, some control in the direction of approved civilized behavior occurs, through most of the approved sentiments, and it is mainly recording of situations of temptation, strong impulsiveness, and the like that the three special source traits come into action.

It needs to be stressed, as Freud did, that the ego treats ethical demands in the same way as any others. It is a-ethical, simply balancing the strength of various demands in the interest of the greatest long-term dynamic satisfactions. Since, in a stable community, "Honesty is the best policy" one would expect the ego to be loaded in the direction of ethical outcomes, but we find this only to a very slight extent (the second order "Control" factor has some C loading). Moreover, though G and Q_3 overlap in some evidences of social attitudes and correlate positively enough to appear in a common second order control factors, $QVIII$, C has only a slight positive loading in $QVIII$. Perhaps it is enough to suggest that the good home background which we posit to be the origin of Q_3 development affects not only G and Q_3 directly, but also provides a dependable background slightly favoring the development of ego strength.

The positive developmental correlation of G and Q_3 and to a lesser degree, C, does not mean that they cannot come into conflict over certain attitudes. Thus, G and Q_3 come into conflict over the worldly view of success and conformity which Q_3 commonly incorporates as self-esteem. This G by Q_3 conflict is expressed by St. Paul: "Those who have to deal with the world should not become engrossed in it" (1 Corinthians 7, 29–31). In contrast with the self-sentiment, which is concerned with social approval, esteem, and success, the superego generally has religious associations and aims at ethical peace with oneself in a deeper sense.

However, on most issues of correct behavior G and Q_3 will be on the same side of the behavioral question, presenting demands to C that it may find difficult to reconcile with lusty ergs and sentiments. Ego strength can be as high in the criminal as in the socially controlled person. It is actually only in the neurotic, the psychotic, and persons in careers that are sheltered from sharp decisionmaking that we find low C values.

Every decision that leads to a gain in long-term satisfaction strengthens the mechanism of the ego by *CR II* conditioning (*ME* Learning). Since each increase in strength favors a better decision in the next occasion of conflict, we would expect a runaway increase in ego strength and abandonment of defense mechanisms. As far as we know, however, the distribution of ego strength scores is pretty well normal so we must recognize events preventing crowding at the top. These situations and events must be the increasing difficulty in process 2 (p. 60) of foreseeing from circumstances how responses to events will turn out. We think of the failures of the eminent and of the Ecclesiastes' comment that success does not invariably come to the wise, but that "... time and circumstances happeneth to them all." However, Heather Cattell (1984) has shown in therapy how training in the processes of ego action can substantially raise the diminished ego strength of neurotics and reduce anxiety. The problem in the neurotic is that the rewards that should have strengthened the ego have been absorbed in defense mechanisms from which the energy of the ego still needs to recoup itself.

Central in all control of impulses are the cognitive stimuli that produce action. The interim and final processes in ego control hinge on the person's capacity to evoke the suitable cognitive stimuli from available engram resources. The martyr facing death at the stake has to evoke visions of paradise. The boy about to steal the ham has to evoke memories of the thrashing he received last time. Cognitive therapy, popular in this decade, is full of observations on the redirection of action by evoked and relearned cognitive connections.

In conflict of two sems or ergs we must therefore expect that it takes place mainly by attempts to control inner and outer cognitive stimuli. The sem that has most ready contact with its inner and outer stimuli is likely to win out. We contact here a process which has its ultimate extreme action in Freudian repression in which all memories that might stimulate a certain course of action are blacked out by the winning sem—normally the ego itself. We then have an isolated dynamic response system that obtains expression only obliquely by consciously unrecognized outlets as a complex.

In considering the control of an antisocial or inappropriate expression we have recognized the role of the second order factor of **control**, representing the general effect of a good family upbringing and loading C, G, Q_3, and F (-). We should pause to note the effect of the last. Desurgency, a general soberness and self control of impulsiveness, appears in this second order factor because the family or cultural pressures favor this restraint as a generalized attitude to life. It aids the pause for immediate control in the action of the ego. It accounts for the quiet in a good restaurant in contrast to the noise in a joint. It means a less naive attitude toward self-expression and desurgency, incidentally is a factor found higher in truly original, creative people (Drevdahl & Cattell, 1958). Thus, there is probably a high preponderance of negative loadings on F in most control.

G, the superego, enters only or mainly into moral decisions. The mystery in G, relative to Q_3, which rewards itself by social approval, is the origin of its quite strong G action without apparant reward. The reward lies in the past: in the fear of loss of love of the parent as a child, who still goes on acting cut-off like a complex from manipulation in adult reward systems. Clearly, this can sometimes get out of hand and the psychotherapist then finds himself trying to cut down to size the superego strength which causes compulsions and depressions.

The self sem (self-sentiment), though, according to loadings, generally following the superego in support of socially approved behavior has a far wider area of controlling action. It pursues worldly success and self esteem. Its beginning lies in adoption of admired characters in the way that Bandura (1962), Inhelder and Piaget (1958), James (1890), McDougall (1932), and others have studied. It leads to anxiety to the extent that the perceived self falls short of the ideal self which probably accounts for much of its negative loading in anxiety, Q_{II}. Any serious discrepancy of the self image and the reality is on the way to what psychoanalysis sees as breakdown of its reality principle. The normal adolescent tries on many masks before finding one that tolerably fits his natural capacities. The finally adopted ideal self-image at the center of Q_3 is what ultimately assists in bringing stability to behavior. It is to the attainment of this self-image that the tactical behavior of the ego, C, is also directed. The states which we see as derived from events with the dynamic structures, issuing as elation, depression, arousal, anxiety, fatigue, etc., constitute a setting within which the ego acts and modifies its actions.

So far we have considered the ego, C, as our main source trait in the behavioral equation. Though we have not been directed to it by any indications in the factor analyses, we may need to consider a change in this model on general grounds. It supposes that the ego acts, not in ordinary interaction with other traits, but **through** them as a modifier of their behavior by direct action on the source traits thus:

$$C' = (b_{ca}A + b_{cb}B + b_{cc}C' + b_{cd}D + \ldots.) \qquad (15\text{-}1)$$

This is one way of fitting the idea that by thinking of the CET (Cattell, 1980—Cue Evocation of Traits) stimulators of various dynamic source traits C brings them into action to achieve the desired long-term satisfactions. At first glance (15-1) might seem to imply that C should appear analytically, not as a primary but as a second order among primaries. However, this cannot be supported because the b weights would presumably be different for each different control interference by C. Nor do we find C, so far, empirically, as a single second order factor but only in Q_{II}, anxiety, among several primaries. There is, in fact, no simple statistical way by which the action of C could be detected as in Equation (15-1) except by an arbitrary comparison of the various b's on primaries in various inhibiting attitude actions, with C held at the same level for all in the group. The remaining questions about control action are better discussed in the next chapter on systems theory.

16   The *VIDAS* Systems Model

We know that most living things require a systems model to explain their action. A systems model is one that takes account of sources of energy and their replacement and of the numerous adjustive feedbacks between one part of the system and others. It usually connotes the idea of stability in a state of homeostasis.

The *VIDA* model has contributed checkable traits, states, and processes, but it has not bound them together in what such writers as Smuts (1926), Koestler (1967), and the gestalt psychologists have asked for as the action of the **whole**, the ghost within the machine. Bertalanphy (1969), Miller (1970), Pribram (1967), Rapaport (1960), Royce and Buss (1976) and Scriven (1963) are among those who have made arguments for systems theory in psychology.

The *VIDAS* theory begins with the simplest system, as frequently stated, in Figure 16–1. Here the essential systems concept is feedback of perception of the results of action to guide the continuing response. It is what happens when we miss the keyhole with the first thrust. It causes **a set of elements, some better called subsystems** in continued interaction to reach a certain goal for the whole system. In living forms, the goal is frequently homeostasis, a return to a comfortable innerstate of satisfaction, but it can be anything—such as solution to an intelligence test, a maximization of absorption of energy from the environment, etc. Systems theorists recognize **open** and **closed** systems. The former has unsettled business remaining with an outer environment while the whole universe is included in the system of the latter. Our treatment of personality with emphasis on the environment belongs to the closed system.

In the *VIDAS* system we begin with the structures discovered and used in the *VIDA* equations and no longer consider the outer stimulus

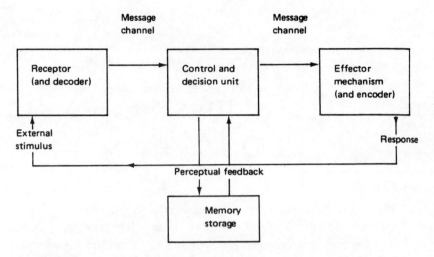

FIGURE 16-1. Basic examples of a behavioral systems model.

triggering a response in a black box organism that operates as a mere transmitter as in reflexology. Instead the stimulus sets in motion several interactions within the box which deny any simple total action stimulus-response law.

The facts and exchanges which the *VIDAS* model finds essential are:

1. reservoirs of information bits or energy which are exhaustible and place limits to individual actions
2. channels serving interactions of sources and limited by varying capacities to carry information
3. the action of reversible and irreversible processes
4. a hierarchical structure in which higher level holons (self-sufficient wholes) exercise control over the behavior of lower levels by cybernetic, guiding action, and
5. the existence of encoding and decoding units mainly between the outer and the inner world.

The last item reminds us of the common development of systems theory and computers in the past forty years. The resources used in the psychobiological system are **information, matter**, and **energy**. Information may be in bits, as in the computer. In physiology, matter may be blood flow, concentrations of hormones, etc. Energy can be physical or psychological, as yet incompletely defined. The last is a concept which psychologists, James, Freud, McDougall, and countless others insist on using but cannot define and measure. In Cattell (1980, p. 429) an operational definition to which there has not been time for an academic response has been attempted but we shall proceed to use the concept of energy.

The systems model uses the entities defined by personality structure research, but it allows for internal reaction among them more varied than the linear, additive relations of the VIDA model, i.e., VIDAS is not based on subjective philosophical concepts from thin air but rests on elements that are the structural outcomes of fifty years of multivariate experimental work.

As Figure 16-2 shows the traits of the VIDAS model are gathered together in eleven major organs. First there is E, the energy source of all ergs, which has a secondary compartment for ergs actually in a state of arousal as a result of stimulation by the perceptual apparatus, P, and the memory, M. The memory source of stored engrams, mainly sems, also has its derivative parts, M, the presently activated sems, and LM, a learning apparatus generating new sems as a result of interaction of M, E, and P. In connection with this we have an extension of the perceptual organ, P, into PD which has the task of evaluating the extent of dynamic reward from various actions undertaken. All these "steps" have already been put into equations above. Finally supervising the E, M, and P interactions is the controlling ego, D, with the help of the general state reservoir, GS, which we have seen to exercise a general direction on the solution of dynamic conflicts. Also acting along with the ego are all the nondynamic traits, T's, which present limiting powers for the ego to take into account.

When the decision on an external act is made by D as a result of the internal processes beginning with the perceptual encoder, P, the act is partly determined in its character by the nondynamic traits, T, which feed into shaping of the act by A, the output determiner.

The most important of the internal processes is an interaction of E and M that we have barely mentioned previously and have handled more fully in Figures 24-1 and 24-2 (pp. 144 and 145). In this engram-drive interaction we envisage the basic dynamic equation:

$$a_{hijk} = \overset{x=p}{\Sigma} b_{bjkx} E_{xi} + \overset{x=q}{\Sigma} b_{bjky} M_{yi} \qquad (16\text{-}1)$$

to be augmented by a product term, EM, thus becoming:

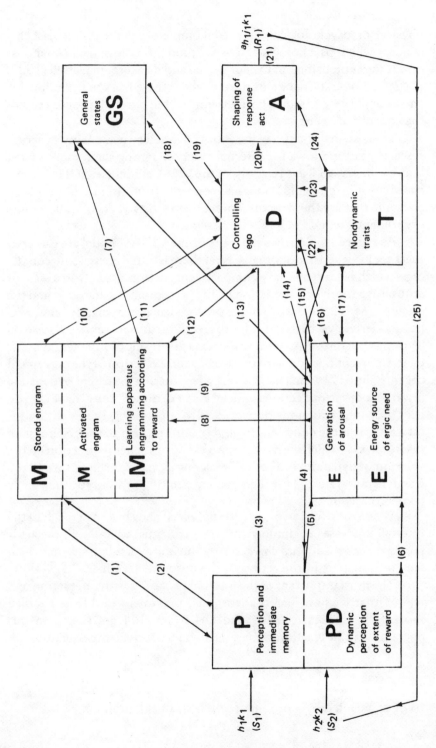

CHANNELS AND RESERVOIRS

(1) Apperception information contributed
(2) Referral to memory bank
(3) Direct information on result of simple motor action
(4) Trait effects on perception
(5) Direct innate stimulation of ergs
(6) Information on reward
(7) Information on reward
(8) Reciprocal action of ergic tension on M activation
(9) Stimulation of ergs by sentiment
(10) Cognitive feedback on final responses and results of earlier experience
(11) Referral to sentiment "committee"
(12) Invocation of controlling cues

(13) Tempering effects of general states on ergs
(14) Action urged by ergic demands
(15) Information on degree of ergic gratification occurring
(16) Invocation of controlling cues
(17) Temperament limitations to arousal
(18) Effect of ego decisions on general states
(19) Effect of general states on ego decisions
(20) Dynamic goal decisions sent for executive action
(21) Emergence of response to stimulus S_1
(22) Sensing fitness of action to ability and temperament traits
(23) Call on abilities to help decision
(24) Temperament-ability endowments shaping effectiveness of response
(25) Response success or failure as new stimulus (S_2) input

FIGURE 16-2. The full *vidas* systems model of personality.

$$a_{hijk} = \overset{x=p}{\underset{}{\sum}} b_{hjkx}E_{xi} + \overset{y=p,\ y=q}{\underset{}{\sum}} b_{hjky}E_{xi}M_{yi} + \overset{y=q}{\underset{}{\sum}} b_{hjky}M_{yi}$$

$$(16\text{-}2)$$

The product EM is actually $EM + ME$, representing two distinct psychological actions as viewed in Figures 24–1 and 24–2. ME represents the action of an activated sentiment as in the second term in Equation (16–1) arousing an erg. If we stand by our position that every ergic arousal other than that due to purely innate stimuli is the result of a learned attachment to part of a sentiment engram, then activation of the sentiment is the common means of arousal of an erg. All ergic arousal comes through stimuli, and these stimuli either have an innate attachment which in Equation (16–2) are represented by b_{hijx} or a semic origin which we contain in $b_{hjkxy}M_{yi}$.

However, we are recently getting experimental evidence that semic engrams conversely get activated by higher ergic tension presences. For example, Shearer (1984) and Boyle (1983) show that a higher state level on a particular erg makes easier the activation of all engrams in any sem through which the erg has been obtaining satisfactions. The arousal of the fear erg, for example, causes readier rise into consciousness and action of the attitudes regarding insurance and health protection. This ergic-semic interaction will be expected regardless of whether the ergic tension rise is due to ulterior environmental stimulation or internal appetitive change though this duality remains to be experimentally checked.

The result in the dynamic behavioral equation is embarrassing because it introduces a process that could run away with itself with seemingly positive feedback. In EM the M is brought to a higher value, and thus in ME the ergic tension is further raised. The limit to this process must be set by the limited availability of ergic tension in relation to competitive uses elsewhere, e.g., in other ergs. Incidentally, though the EM product can be given a single weight as in Equation (16–2), it would probably be best to split it into two terms, each with its own weight thus:

$$\Sigma b_{hjkxy}E_{xi}M_{yi} = \Sigma b_{hjkxy}E_{xi}M_{yi} + \Sigma b_{hykyx}M_{yi}E_{xi}$$

$$(16\text{-}3)$$

Here we encounter a difference of the *VIDA* and *VIDAS* models in the

E and M values used. If we enter E_{xi} and the M_{yi} values we normally score for individual i, as in the VIDA model, these values will almost immediately be changed by the VIDAS interaction to new, higher values. This is but one example of the effects of the internal interaction which the systems model calls us to recognize. The separate E and M, first and last terms in VIDAS Equation (16–2) must also be altered according to the interaction effect, to conform with values in the middle term.

Thus, the diagram in Figure 16–2, with interactions of only eleven elements can get quite complex, and each internal interaction calls for its own equation to settle values before we insert them in the final behavioral equation. In the case of the above intervention of E's and M's with p E's and q M's, it is evident that the product must be a matrix one in which every E interacts appropriately with every M, i.e., the middle term is actually the sum of p and q products (Figure 24–1).

The unravelling of what happens in a system from knowledge of only what is fed into it and what behavior emerges, promises to be extremely complex. Theoretically, from enough cases and enough behaviors, one can factor analytically find the number of internal influences at work; but since we now realize that their nature is not simply additive, this is nothing more than an approximation. For example, if we factor behaviors determined by Equation (16–2), ought we not to obtain either three classes of factors or even $p + q + pq$ factors since the action of each pq is presumably different? In fact, by ordinary factor results, we continue to find only $(p + q)$ factors, the products being treated as **sums** of p and q effects as is known to occur in many product relations in factor analysis approximations.

Here we cannot pursue further the disentanglement of the influence and their interaction in Figure 16–2, which involves specialized mathematics, but whenever an approximate theory is reached it can be tested today by putting it into a computer and testing its truth by **computer simulation**. It is probable that further understanding of the VIDAS model will have to come by such trial-and-error study of particular theories of internal interactions. Meanwhile we have a model that fits most of what we know and that can be pursued into the study of processes.

17   The Social, Group Behavior
        Aspects of Dynamics

We have recognized that the *VIDAS* theory is of an open system—open between the individual and the individual's environment. This being evident, no prediction of individual behavior is possible without knowing what goes on in the environment, which we may take here as being the social environment.

Every individual belongs to a number of groups so we need to begin by recognizing their nature. A group is an assembly of individuals gathered together for satisfying the needs of its individuals. It is a means and a device and lasts as long as it can continue to supply ergic needs.

Since the dynamic needs attitude, "I want to belong to this group," can be stated in an equation for each person, we can get a sum of these equations to express what we will call the total **synergy** of each given group thus:

$$S_E = \overset{i=n}{\underset{}{\sum}}\overset{x=b}{\underset{}{\sum}} b_{bjkx}E_{xi} + \overset{i=n}{\underset{}{\sum}}\overset{xy=bg}{\underset{}{\sum}} b_{bjkxy}E_{xi}M_{yi} + \overset{i=n}{\underset{}{\sum}}\overset{y=c}{\underset{}{\sum}} b_{bjky}M_{yi}$$

$$(17\text{--}1)$$

The synergy, S_E, might be expressed partly in the size of subscriptions to the group, partly in work done for and in it. The synergy of a group is a vector quality that in addition to its total strength (length in a diagram), tells us the **quality** of the satisfaction of ergs and sems in each.

If we suppose that most human satisfactions come from groups, then there is a competition among groups for members and their appetitive needs such that an enlargement of satisfaction in one group implies a necessary loss of population or synergy in others. These readjustments tell us much about history, e.g., the European switch from the Holy Roman Empire to separate nationalities in the sixteenth and seventeenth centuries, and some switch from the family to state services in our own time.

The characteristics by which different groups are to be described can be obtained by factoring social indicators and with modern nations as subjects this leads to approximately twenty factorial traits. Of these cultural pressure, size, affluence, degree of industrialization, morality level, and others have been defined and rendered measurable. A profile of scores on these yields a description of national **syntality** equivalent to personality in an individual and capable of (a) predicting many behaviors and (b) by profile similarity measures permitting nations to be classified in a dozen types representing civilizations (in Toynbee's sense). Figure 17-1 shows some profile means after objectively grouping nations by profiles.

In general, we can see that syntality is a product of the characteristics of the population, P, and the cultural structure, C, thus:

$$S = (f)P \cdot C \qquad (17\text{-}2)$$

though this equation is presently far from being derived in actual cases.

The C value in Equation (17-2) includes the role structure of individuals, the forms of government and religion, and all that is handed on by tradition. The P has both acquired and innate, racial trait bases. That a role is a detectable dynamic structure in factored behavior has already been discussed. It is also sociologically definable as a set of ties to other people by frequency of contact or delivery of messages and as a set of expectations that people have of a given type of person.

Much of sociology has to deal with establishing the network of ties that enable us to recognize structures. The psychologist would want to establish the ties not merely by events of interaction frequences but also by the dynamic vector of the ties as judged by the attitude of one person to another.

A special mode of research is to compare the syntality which includes synergy of a group **with and without** the presence of a particular person. If we operationally define a leader as the person whose presence alters the syntality of a group most, we have here the most positive basis for locating real leaders.

Among important group phenomena is that of group learning (Cattell, 1953). Some group structures, e.g., those with a leader, make most learning more rapid. What slows group learning relative to indi-

Objectively Located Dimensions of National Culture

Cultural Dimensions, Measured as Factors

Factor 1: Size

Factor 2: Cultural pressure versus direct ergic expression

Factor 3: Enlightened affluence versus narrow poverty

Factor 4: Conservative patriarchal solidarity versus ferment of release

Factor 5: Emancipated urban rationalism versus unsophisticated stability

Factor 6: Thoughtful industriousness versus emotionality

Factor 7: Vigorous, self-willed order versus unadapted perseveration

Factor *8: Bourgeois Philistinism versus reckless bohemianism

Factor 9: Residual or peaceful progressiveness

Factor 10: Fastidiousness versus forcefulness

Factor 11: Buddhism-Mongolism

Factor 12: Poor cultural integration and morale versus good internal morality

Objectively Discovered Types in Cultural Patterns

Contrast of Central Tendencies in Three Culture Patterns[a]

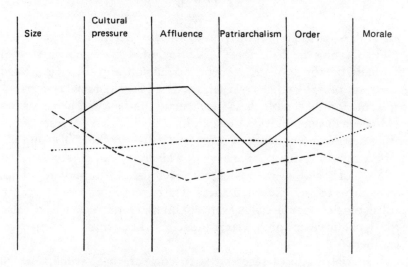

KEY: _____ The American-British-Australian Pattern

_ _ _ _ _ _ The China-India-Liberia Pattern

.... The Russia-Argentina-Arabia Pattern

[a]The vertical scale is in standard score units for each factor, but is not set out numerically.

FIGURE 17-1. Central type tendencies in national syntality profiles.

viduals is that (a) it is difficult to get the group reward in learning back to the individuals responsible for the learning and (b) much group learning requires quite complex coordinations of action by **many** individuals, involving changes of role and structure as well as individual learning. It is not surprising that such learning is slow and erratic.

Another important group phenomenon is the rise of class distinction. It has been shown in a comparison of many occupations that their social status emerges as a general factor loading the average intelligence in the occupation, the average salary, the size of house, the prestige rating of the occupation, and a number of other variables commonly voiced as signs of status. Status is a motivating reality in individual ambition, and it is interesting to find that actual prestige and intelligence load the social status factor more than earnings, etc. (Cattell, 1942).

As the subject of research social dynamics is still in its infancy, but the broad outlines of what needs to be studied have been outlined above. We need to know the syntality and synergy vectors of many groups before we can predict the joining and leaving behavior of most individuals. It becomes necessary also to know the dynamic lattices of groups, the subsidiations in the behavior of which are as real as those of individuals. A worker belongs, for example, to a sports team which subsidiates in part to a political party, and so perhaps to a religious group, etc.

The application of the dynamic calculus to group life has clear principles both for the individual's attitudes to this group and that and for the rise and fall of groups in interaction. The main generalizations, however, must depend on the progress of experimentation with dynamic measures of the belonging attitudes involved.

18   Two Theories on the Nature
of Motivation Components

Having followed the measurement of dynamic traits from their first structuring to their interaction in systems theory and group life, we must pause to look at some unsolved problems set aside as we progressed, beginning with objective motivation measurement.

In the first place we need better definition of the main primaries, α, β, γ, δ, etc., and of the U and I secondary factors in motivation measurement devices. R-technique studies have been pretty thoroughly replicated, but we lack adequate P- and dR-technique studies to clarify the force of these factors as **states** for motivation measures should depend largely on **state** measures, and it is possible that some variables, e.g., those using information, are too traitlike to measure passing dynamic states.

More experimentation is needed not only on the list of specific devices loaded on each primary but also on the relation of primary to life criterion measures such as time and money spent on a course of action. The consciously expressed verbal interest in a course of action shows substantial loading on α and γ but virtually nothing on the other primaries. This raises a question to be answered only by P- and dR-technique experiments whether the other primaries may not be traits, not particularly connected with motivation. On the other hand, the latter do not correlate with other personality traits as might be expected and they **do** show a correlation with achievement that would be expected of an interest strength (Cattell & Butcher, 1968).

Until such experiments are done we see U as an id-based, wishful-thinking interest, perhaps indicating the direction in which interest is trying to get real expression. By contrast, β, showing fantasy, projection, and preference loadings, is still clearly connected with accomplished expression of interest in information about and study of an interest, with speed of warming up also being well loaded. It is well expressed as ego interest with predominance of cognitive memory and perception. γ has been called superego interest, but it has more in it than "I ought to be interested in this." It has selective perception, word association, autism, and thoughts on the ultimate utility of the course of action. It shows strong conscious involvement, again with an egolike quality but additionally with regard for a social importance of the course of action. This may be akin to the persistance and social obligation that appear in superego ratings.

The delta factor loads little but hidden figures, persistence, speed of decision, especially retroactive inhibition, and the physiological measures of GSR, and small blood pressure change. Because it alone loads the latter, it has been considered the physiological factor in interest; however, it has an in-depth quality to its interference (retroactive inhibition) and its penetration in hidden figures, which also suggest some will power. It must stay uninterpreted until more devices are tried out to designate it.

The epsilon, ϵ, factor, negatively loads memory effects—cues and reminiscenses—and criterion utility, GSR response, persistence, and time and money spent positively. The combination of poor memory for the interest with large GSR fits Ikin, Pear and Thouless's (1924) definition of a complex, but the pattern also has the character of a practical interest devoid of any deeper attachment, with a slight superego contribution. We tentatively hold to the term complex or id, meaning an interest sustained by superficial arguments and associations but actually of more fundamental real origin.

We come next to a factor, zeta, ζ, that is not too well confirmed across the Cattell et al. (1978) and the Cattell and Child (1975) patterns. It loads muscle tension at decision and speed of decision with some negative loadings on fluency and hidden figures. It may be confined in high loadings just to speed and vigor of decision.

The seventh factor, eta, η, checks well across studies and loads persistence, fluency on cues, consequences, and word association, warm-up, and hidden figures. It has a quality of attentiveness not unlike γ, with which its pattern has a substantial, pattern, –42, similarity coefficient.

Finally, the Cattell, McGill, et al. (1978) study located an eighth factor, theta, θ, with a loading on quick warm-up but reduced speed of decision, which perhaps bespeaks an indurated component of interest of no great conscious importance.

As stated earlier in Chapter 1, these factors stand up across quite different attitude **contents**. As yet no substantial correlations have been found with personality factors, though we feel that we can see such connections, notably in β being an ego source and γ, a superego expansion. However, since a preliminary P-technique shows these patterns, it seems that they are not personality traits as such. It is of theoretical interest that seven primary factors have also been found in the factoring of numerous motivation strength measures in rats running mazes (Cattell and Dielman, 1974).

A promising attempt has been alternatively made to identify them with the influences in the hypothetical formula for ergic tension (p. 29) in which it is supposed that the alignment is as in Table 18–1. This deals with a formulation for the seven motivation components in an attitude that we have not previously fully set out as follows:

$$a_{bijk} = bE^1 + bE^{11} + s_{ke}E_1 + s_{km}ME + s_kM$$
$$+ (s_{km}M{-}M) + (s_{ke}EM{-}M) \tag{18-1}$$

It derives from the ergic tension formula in that E^1 and E^{11} respectively represent the nonappetitive and the appetitive parts of the drive strength. The remaining symbols represent the arousal and activation, spelled out separately for E and M and the ME and EM products. As Figure 18–1 shows the argument is that the physiological id interest, E, is considered to equal $(C + H + I)$, the drive part, E^1. The physiological viscerogenic, appetitive part E^{11} we consider identifiable as δ. The ergic arousal, $S_{ke}E$ the innate ergic part, we match with zeta, ζ, which has the character of a simple vigor. The engram strength of the unaroused sem, M, we equate with the cognitively emphatic, β component, etc. The last two terms are speculatively matched with the last two in Table 18–1.

It is understood that Figure 18–1 represents a speculative theory for which there is as yet no evidence save for the fit of the loadings of the primaries to the concepts put forward. The matter could be investigated by taking two or three ergic attitude measurements under different degrees of physiological need and external stimulation and comparing the primary scores. However, Table 18–1 and Equation 18–1 constitute the principal alternative hypothesis or components to that adduced earlier.

As we turn from primaries to secondary motivation factors we see a distribution of primaries as in Figure 1–1, p. 5. A good deal of clinical and general evidence on these factors has already accumulated, especially through use of the MAT and SMAT, the practical standardized measuring

TABLE 18-1. Hypothesis on Relation of Seven Motivation Components to Phases in Erg-Sentiment Action

1. Constitutional need strength with non-viscerogenic appetite*	E'	(ϵ)
2. Viscerogenic component in need strength	E''	(δ)
3. Arousal of erg from innate cognative paths	$s_{k\theta}E = E_1$	(ξ)
4. Arousal of erg through sentiment activation	$s_{km}ME = E_2$	(η)
5. Engram strength of sentiment as such	M	(β)
6. Activation of engram by environment directly	$s_{km}M-M = M_1$	(ν)
7. Activation of sentiment through ergic tension	$s_k EM-M = M_2$	(α)

*It is possible to conceive of a split in the need strength in two or three ways according to equation. One would be put to the appetitive part (in the square brackets) in a category different from the fixed constitutional. Here, guided by indications of some separateness of the physiological appetite we have put this viscerogenic part (P-G$_p$) separately as E''. Thus $E=E'+E''$, but this split is probably not relevant to the products of E such as 3, $s_{k\theta}E$ and 7, $s_{k\theta}EM$.

devices used clinically and in business. We have raised the question of whether the I measure should not be higher in sems than in ergs. The question is difficult to answer experimentally because the attitudes to be compared have to be different in content. However, with as many as half a dozen attitude contents taken at random for an erg and for a sem, consistent results would probably appear.

The more clinically vital issue is how far the score $(U - I)$ represents degrees of conflict in the ergic or semic area concerned in the measurement. The results definitely show that an excess of undischarged, U need, over integrated, expressed need, I, generally but not invariably assesses conflict and maladaptation in the area. It is not invariable because sometimes a low $(U - I)$ value apparently means that a large I value has been built up with resulting reduction of U by, for example, a more elderly person in whom the drive itself, U, has come to the end of its interest, leaving I as purely intellectual, physiologically—unsustained interest. The work of Sweney & Cattell (1961), Heather Cattell (1984), Krug (1969), Anton (1984), Shearer (1984), and others has resulted in many interesting new generalizations about the indications of ergic and semic strength measures. Woliver and Cattell (1984) also have shown that in married couples the MAT scores in each dynamic trait are positively correlated across the couples.

The field next needs a separate study of the second order factors across the ten measurable dynamic structure factors for U and I. The problem of interpreting correlations is the existence of spurious negative covariance through half the U and half the I subtest scores being ipsative. Brennan and Cattell (1984) have recently shown that the distortion in factoring ipsative scores can be reduced to trivial proportions, so where this correction is applied we can raise the question of whether there is a single power behind all the ergs as discussed in the next chapter. Meanwhile, we would assume that the total interest-energy of each person will run as a general factor through all U measures, fixing each person at a different total energy.

A number of other relations would be expected with U and I scores. First, we should expect I investments to increase with age, much as remembered coping skills wax in the growth through life of crystallized intelligence (Cattell, 1981). Second, we should expect a correlation of ego strength, C, with total I score. This has already been indicated in results, as also has a correlation of about 0.5 between C and **stability**, averaged over all of many attitudes, when retested for strength after an interval (Cattell, 1943; Das, 1955). (Note that other personality factors, notably extraversion and surgency (F) and premsia (I) also show (Wessman & Ricks, 1966) correlation with changeability.) The relation of C to internal logical inconsistency of attitudes (Festinger's cognitive dissonance (1962)), was also shown to be highly significant (negatively) by Cattell and Warburton (1967). Incidentally, psychological internal consistency, judged on logical content, should not be confused with a high homogeneity coefficient. It has been shown (Cattell, 1982b) that the measures of particular ergic tensions and sem levels show quite low internal homogeneity (Cooper & Kline, 1982), which is what is psychologicall required because one must sample expressions of the erg as widely as possible.

From the above it is evident that in such tests as the MAT and $SMAT$ we are measuring motivation strength objectively and with good criteria predictions, but that the nature of the eight primaries, α, β, γ, etc., is still a matter of comparative speculation. The U and I second orders seem better understood and their clinical meaning and use is already considerable. More objective devices need to be invented, directed to the two main theories about primaries, and tested by suitable techniques to clarify the origins of primaries.

19   Exploration Needed on Properties of Ergs and Sems

With the use of tested **motivation component** measures the time is now ripe for further exploration of dynamic structure factors among attitudes. The list of indicated human ergs (p. 9) is tolerably complete as regards the main drives, but there are numerous suspected innate patterns awaiting discovery and definition. Similarly, in the semic area the sociology and social psychology of cultures calls for a more complete map of the principal sems in our culture than that yet reached (p. 13).

It is clear that the dynamic structure factors are the same no matter which devices, α or β, U or I, are used for measurement. A factor analytic phenomenon that occurs here, however, is that there is sometimes the possibility of alternative solutions as shown in Table 19-1. Here in this simple example the usual slight uncertainty over numbers of factors to be extracted from the measurement of 14 attitudes by one U and one I device. The result can be expressed either as three factors, each combining the devices with the dynamic structure factors or as in Table 19-1 in five factors with some variance of the vehicle drives in separate factors. Foreseeably, the latter has the true weight on the attitudes, but in practice we commonly do not separate the vehicle variance from the substantive variance and thus get somewhat higher correlations among the attitudes than really exist and some vehicle mixture contaminating the actual scores.

It seems that the highest loadings on an ergic factor are commonly on attitudes nearer in the lattice to the goal. Thus, we should expect sentiment factors to be more distal in the lattice from the ergic consummatory goals; and since we have proposed that the integrity of the self-sentiment is a precondition for most other sentiment satisfaction, we should expect the self-sem to be most distal of all. These theories can

TABLE 19-1. Relation of Simple Structure Dynamic Structure Factor to Instrument Factors in Objective Devices

		Factor Matrix			
	Psychological Factors			Instrument Factors	
Attitude Variable and Device Measurement	Escape Erg	Sentiment to Parents	Self-Sentiment	Information Device Factor	Autism Device Factor
1 Desire for good self-control. Information measure	00	-02	[26]	[54]	03
2 Wish to know oneself. Information measure	03	-05	[31]	27	19
3 Wish never to become insane. Information measure	-06	12	[22]	43	04
4 Readiness to turn to parents for help. Information measure	-02	[35]	09	28	-01
5 Feeling proud of one's parents. Information measure	-06	[28]	-01	24	01
6[a] Desire to avoid fatal disease and accidents. Inforamtion measure	16	04	13	[65]	-02
7[a] Wish to get protection form A bomb. Information measure	[14]	-08	03	[14]	-05
8 Desire for good self-control. Autism measure	01	-04	[30]	02	[22]
9 Wish to know oneself. Autism measure	-08	07	[37]	-01	[31]
10 Wish never to become insane. Autism measure	00	-01	16	00	[25]
11 Readiness to turn to ones parents for help. Autism measure	-08	[18]	09	-08	[42]
12 Feeling proud of ones parents. Autism measure	-03	[14]	01	06	[14]
13[a] Desire to avoid fatal disease and accidents. Autism measure	[26]	20	01	04	[17]
14[a] Wish to get protection from A bomb. Autism measure	[23]	13	09	15	[10]

Note–The theoretically required salients to define the factors are boxed in, and except for two values at the bottom of the parental sentiment factor column, the salients are high (above .13) where, and only where, they are theoretically required to be.

[a] Attitudes 13 and 14 are the same as 6 and 7, but in a different medium, and similarly, for the other cross-media personality factors.

be most readily checked by the blocking method of tracing subsidiations (p. 17).

By the hydraulic model we should expect the strength of attitudes in a single chain to be the same at all points, but simple chains are very rare. Commonly we should experiment with the expectation that the sum of attitude strengths will be the same as the main trunk when a branching occurs. The hydraulic model presumably applies to *need* strength measures because the ergic tension arousal, even in a simple chain (Figure 13-3, p. 77), will vary with the closeness of the goal and with the stimulation of subgoals. If the theoretical alignment of Table 18-1 in Chapter 18 should be supported, we could then use the various processes to separate ergic tension, drive, need, and other components in the investigation of the lattice.

Incidentally, the role of the M and EM terms (Equation 16-2, p. 96) in the measurement of an attitude strength has been theoretically assigned, respectively, to the β, γ, and α factors, which are well represented in the MAT subtests in motivation devices. However, these strengths of the M derivatives are strictly *cognitive*, not dynamic (except ME in γ, etc.), and so should be omitted, if possible, from a measure of the **dynamic** strength of an attitude. The dynamic component in the total attitude strength is

$$a_{hijk(d)} = b_{hjke'}E_i' + b_{hjke''}E_i'' + b_{hjkr'}E_{1i} + b_{hjkn}E_{ni}$$

$$(19-1)$$

which corresponds very closely to the second order U component and could test our hypothesis that this measure should be strongest in measures of ergic factors.

Experiments began a decade ago on attempts to show that artificial stimulation (changes in U) could produce the changes in ergic tension that could theoretically be expected from the model. The experiments include both external stimuli in the case of fear and internal appetite in the case of hunger. The results of Adelson (1952), Cattell and Barton (1974), DeYoung et al. (1973), Cattell, Kawash, and DeYoung (1972) and Krug (1971) showed that either or both of the U and I components altered as expected for fear, sex, and hunger. The changes were on unintegrated fear (rising also during the day), and higher in unintegrated than integrated sex (positively correlated with actual sex activity within 24 hours), and also on both U and I in hunger. They clearly show that both external and internal causes produce change in ergic tension, as expected from our formula (p. 27) and shown by the fact that in dR- and

P- techniques the ergs and sems change in the same unitary pattern as in R-technique.

The theory that any basic drive strength varies from person to person and expresses itself **either** in U or in I forms explains the virtual zero correlation of U and I across people while requiring a more inverse correlation in P-technique which so far has been observed in slight degree and awaits further experiment. The sems, it will be remembered, also show up in dR- and P-techniques, but only one experiment has yet been undertaken empirically to show that stimulation of one attitude on a sem produces change in all (Krug, 1971). Since the sem unity is acquired in stages, we may well expect its activation to appear less as a whole than occurs in the arousal of an erg.

A grossly neglected issue in dynamics is the proof of differentiation of ergs from sems by their greater heritability. This heritability applies to the drive component, which can be measured either by taking an average score for people across several situations and appetitive states or if theory agrees by taking only epsilon (ϵ) component measures. The genetic analysis for heritability would follow by $MAVA$ or twin techniques (Cattell, 1981). (Note that we should not expect ordinary sem measures (but only those above, p. 107) to be completely free of hereditary action because the dynamic investment in the sem is ergic in nature. Only the M part should prove largely environmental.)

There remains, as indicated above, a great deal of research to be done on sems and their learning growth. First, there is need for further research than Sweney and Cattell's (1961) on the age development of semic structure in children. What **is** the structure of sems typically at five and ten years of age for example? The present evidence is that it is relatively fragmentary, with many small sems that organize themselves with age into clearer groupings. The proportion of ergic energy in sems must be low initially and steadily increase with age. This should be demonstrable also by changes in the motivation components in a representative sample of attitudes.

The three hypothesized forms of sem growth by **uniform conditioning** of attitudes, **budding**, and **aids** need experimental checking. Dielman and the present writer attempted to show the first by rat experiments. The equivalent of sems were different mazes to which the rats were submitted with the same ergic motivations, to very different degrees of learning. It was hypothesized that by taking measures on performance on different parts of each maze we should find factors appearing like human sems after a whole, in proportion to the amount of learning given in each maze. These results have so far not passed the point of the demonstration of the seven motivation component factors, as described above (Cattell & Dielman, 1974, p. 17).

Meanwhile, with humans all three modes of growth could be examined by factoring of the same group of children at relatively short time periods and comparisons made of the individual changes with known institutional impacts from the environment. This has been done in superego measures by Cattell and Carter (1985), but not on sems generally.

The next important area of sentiment study is that relating various phenomena connected with their relative strengths. In the first place can we verify that the frustration of a sem brings anger and depression proportional to its ergic investment? Ethical considerations preclude our interfering with major sems, but we can watch life events and measure the change on emotional state measures as changes, bereavements, promotions, etc. occur with sems of directly measured strengths. The hypothetical expectation would be that anger and depression (usually in that sequence) would be proportional to the ergic investment in the given sem.

Incidentally, though we described the calculation of the **ergic investment** in a sem we gave no attention to the reciprocal calculation of what might be called the **sem mandate** of an erg. Every erg in a settled culture is achieving its satisfaction through several sems, and its mandate can be written as the vector of satisfactions it gets through the various sems. Reciprocally to the investment the mandate calculation comes as the summed product of the ergic and semic loadings in the attitudes sufficiently loaded on the erg and on sems. The semic and ergic values thus add to the same total overall.

20   Light from a Revolution
in Applied Psychology

Many questions that merit discussion remain at the practical, clinical, and applied levels. Both the clinical and the industrial fields are severely in need of the dynamic specification equations for all kinds of behavior with which they have to deal daily. There are specification weights (Cattell & Butcher, 1968) for a number of educational achievements that can be applied by anyone familiar with the behavioral equation. For example, we have (Cattell & Butcher, 1968, p. 215):

Achievement in $= 0.44SE - 0.23SA + 0.37SS - 0.15$ Sex $- 0.24$
School Grades   Fear $+ 0.21$ Pug. $- 0.33$ Narc. $+ 0.36$ Constr.

$$(20-1)$$

where SE = superego, SA = self-assertiveness, SS = self-sentiment, etc. and so on through five ergs. This yields an R of close to 0.5 with the classroom achievement without the addition of personality factors and abilities which raise the multiple R to about 0.75.

In the clinical field we would like the equations showing the likelihood of clinical improvement with this, that, and the other treatment; the likelihood of an alcoholic responding; the danger of suicide; the expected recovery of a depressive; the chances of resolution of a marital problem; etc. With a little organization among clinicians it should be possible to obtain some better than chance predictive b's in these behavioral equations.

The problem of assignment to DSM categories by dynamic structure factor scores is also important. In the **Taxonome** computer program and the pattern similarity coefficient, r_p, we have the means for finding objectively what typological DSM categories actually exist in nature and

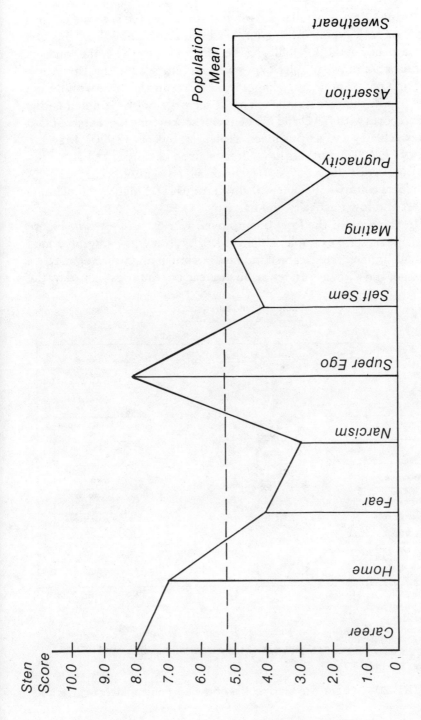

FIGURE 20-1. MAT profile from 30 schizophrenics.

calculating just how similar a given individual profile is to the control profile of each type. Nothing has yet been done along these lines by psychiatrists, but the possibility has become wide open since the concepts of **homostat** and **segregate types** were developed and the Taxonome computer program set up to handle cases. Presumably, one would use a wider profile than that on the ten MAT factors alone by supplementing the ten scores with CAQ and life behavior scores for a more stable DSM than psychiatry has yet produced. However, Sweney (1970), May and Sweney (1965) and others have already given us central MAT profiles for a number of clinical types psychiatrically diagnosed. That for schizophrenics is shown in Figure 20-1. It is unusual in high parental home interest and low pugnacity and narcism.

In the type of the long unemployed worker as shown in Figure 20-2, one sees, for example, a high insecurity (fear erg), a low integrated and high unintegrated career interest, a similar high discrepancy on superego, and a low assertiveness such as can be readily explained by the

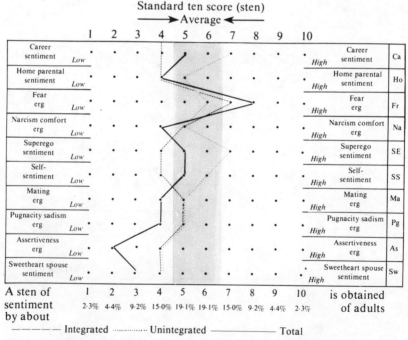

Motivational patterns of the chronically unemployed
Source: Lawlis (1967).

FIGURE 20-2. The dynamic profile of the long unemployed.

circumstances. The three most constant associations of low employability are low integrated career interest, high fear score, and low self-assertion.

A very contrasting vector for presidents of insurance and service organizations is shown in Figure 20-3. Here we see higher interest in career with considerable interest in the self (narcism and self-sentiment) and lower interest in the home. This profile fits clinical evaluations well except for the very low unintegrated superego score. We must suppose that constant concern with the tactics of getting things done and cutting corners has reduced the desire for strong superego action, leaving its emphasis in the overt integrated area. Other executive profiles agree with the above, adding lower than average interest in home and wife. The latter suggests that a single total energy underlies all dynamic structure factors so that eminence in some areas implies that there must be reduction in others. The ipsative scoring of half the tests is not enough to account for this artificially.

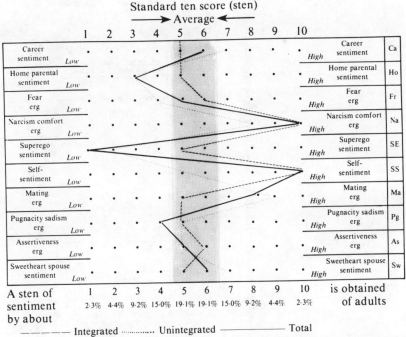

Average scores for top executives (20 presidents of insurance and service organizations)

Source: Unpublished work by C. Noty.

FIGURE 20-3.   The dynamic profile of executives.

MAT results for officer cadet candidates and biserial correlations with selection criterion

MAT Scale	Total group (N=36)		Selected (N=17)		Rejected (N=17)		r_{bis}
	M	SD	M	SD	M	SD	
Career	17.2	2.4	18.3	2.5	16.6	2.4	.33*
Home/parental	17.4	2.5	16.8	2.2	19.0	2.3	-.41†
Fear	11.3	2.4	10.0	2.1	12.0	2.6	-.39†
Narcism	11.2	2.7	10.4	2.5	11.4	2.7	-.18
Superego	31.9	3.8	31.4	4.5	33.0	3.4	-.20
Self-sentiment	51.1	4.8	52.2	5.0	51.5	4.5	.07
Mating	13.2	2.9	13.4	2.5	13.7	3.5	-.05
Pugnacity	12.8	2.5	13.0	2.3	13.3	2.6	-.06
Self-assertion	14.1	3.4	15.3	3.2	13.3	3.8	.28*
Sweetheart-spouse	14.2	2.4	14.2	2.6	13.7	2.1	.10

*Significant at 5% level.
†Significant at 1% level.
These r's are over the total group.

MAT scores for recruit, officer cadet candidates selected and non-commissioned officer course groups

MAT scale	A Recruits (N=138)		B OCS selected (N=17)		C Returned to NCO course (N=35)		t A-B	A-C	B-C
	M	SD	M	SD	M	SD			
Career	16.4	2.7	18.3	2.5	17.6	2.0	2.82†	2.93‡	.98
Home/parental	17.7	3.5	16.8	2.2	17.5	3.4	1.30	.31	.88
Fear	12.7	3.1	10.0	2.1	12.3	2.6	4.09‡	.53	2.46‡
Narcism	10.5	2.7	10.4	2.5	12.5	2.6	.24	4.00‡	2.44‡
Superego	29.7	4.6	31.4	4.5	27.6	4.4	1.44	2.47‡	2.81‡
Self-sentiment	49.5	6.2	52.2	5.0	49.4	4.1	2.02	.11	1.95
Mating	14.7	3.6	13.4	2.5	13.1	2.5	1.86	2.96‡	.34
Pugnacity	12.8	3.5	13.0	2.3	15.2	2.8	.31	4.62‡	2.18*
Self-assertion	12.6	2.9	15.3	3.2	13.5	2.6	3.29‡	2.30	1.77
Sweetheart-spouse	16.2	3.7	14.2	2.6	14.5	3.0	2.78*	2.21*	.32

*Significant at 5% level.
†Significant at 2% level.
‡Significant at 1% level.

FIGURE 20-4. The dynamic profile of face-to-face group leaders.

Except for the profile of leaders in Figure 20-4, in social psychology little of the potential use of measures of dynamic structures has been made. Practically all that we spoke of above (Chapter 14) regarding calculations on group synergy is a wide-open field for experiment. Regarding this profile in Figure 20-4, for small group leaders (officer cadets) it is evident that selection is for high career, low fear, high narcism, high self-sem, high superego, and high self-assertion. We can well imagine these fit the person with the independent spirit, high dependability demanded of the leader (see Figure 20-5).

We have seen that most dynamic traits are susceptible to change. In connection with leadership it is interesting to compare the significant changes shown to occur over a four-year period (18–22) in those gaining job promotions. Figure 20-6 expresses these changes for certain 16PF factors, which can be psychologically understood to some extent,

MAT sten scores (rounded) for various occupational groups

Occupation	N	Career	Home	Fear	Narcism	Superego	Self-sent.	Mating	Pugnacity	Assertion	Sweetheart
Army Officers	44	6	4	5	8	4	5	6	7	5	6
Theological seminary males (clergymen)	279	5	4	4	6	6	6	5	5	4	6
Teachers	64	5	3	5	3	5	7	6	5	5	6
Physicians	112	6	3	6	8	6	7	5	6	5	4
Executives	20	6	3	5	10	1	10	8	4	5	6
Disabled workers	34	6	5	6	5	6	4	5	5	4	5
Construction workers	17	8	4	5	6	4	5	4	7	7	6
Engineer supervisors	27	7	5	5	5	5	5	5	5	5	5
Engineers	23	7	5	5	5	5	5	5	5	6	6
College students	10	5	4	5	3	4	4	3	4	4	4
Chronically unemployed	75	5	4	8	4	5	5	4	4	2	3
Violent criminals	19	5	4	7	3	5	5	2	5	5	3
Nonviolent criminals	19	5	5	5	3	5	5	3	5	4	4
Schizophrenics	30	8	4	4	3	8	4	5	2	5	5

FIGURE 20-5. The dynamic profiles of occupations.

e.g., in Q_3, self-sentiment, and in MAT scores. Those promoted show somewhat greater decline in dominance and a decidedly greater decline in guilt-proneness (unworthiness) and ergic tension; the unpromoted show negligible change in self-sentiment (Q_3) and shrewdness (N), the promoted increase markedly in these.

Such findings also increase our understanding of the source traits. For example, the self-sem increases with success especially in a social sense which fits all we know about it. On the other hand, the increase in shrewdness (versus naivete), N, is unexpected but again makes sense when we realize the greater predicaments in which the promoted person is placed. The declines in guilt-proneness and the frustration present in ergic tension, Q_4, also fit dynamic theory. Thus, social and practical use of dynamic structure measures, duly continued, offer great promise at the more theoretical levels of understanding of treatment.

We can best help understand the synergy of groups by indicating experiments needed to test theories. The sum total of energy given to a group by its members is the total of the individual "I want to belong..." attitudes which may differ according to status and position in the group. What we need are experiments examining the relation of these sums to the power and particular actions of the group. The ergic quality of the summed attitudes need not tell us directly about the ergic quality of the group action since money, which can be given in connection with any attitude, can be converted by group government to any use. However, **some** relation will exist since members will not want to belong to a group differing in effective goals from their own.

The obtaining of certain satisfactions in a group by a given person will reduce the need to join any other group for those satisfactions. The sum of group-belonging attitudes will tend to add up to the total individual's ergic needs. Thus, relations will appear among groups representing the flow of alternative group satisfactions in individuals. The blocking of a satisfaction of a particular ergic quality in one will create a demand for its satisfaction by others. Thus, groups experience a mode of mutually competing that is quite different from direct struggles over world objectives that take place among them elsewhere, also the intrapsychic conflicts in individuals are partly group affiliative in nature mimicking the rivalries of groups, e.g., the family, the business, and sports club.

The synergy that goes into a group is used partly in simply maintaining the group in existence, **maintenance synergy**, and partly in sustaining outside activities, **effective synergy**. The effective synergy

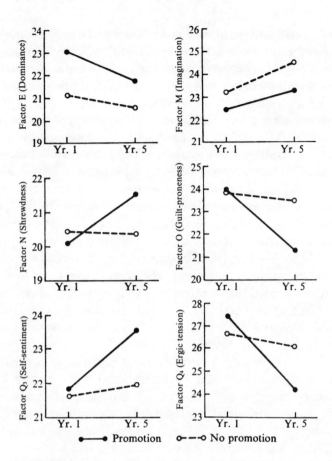

Promotion versus no promotion, occuring between year 1 and year 5 of testing.
Source: Barton and Cattell (1972b).

FIGURE 20-6. Effect of promotion on dynamic personality factors.

may be given to research, to military defense, to missionary work, etc. The ratio of effective-to-maintenance synergy can tell us a lot about the group. The individual's attitude "I want to belong..." likewise also covers satisfactions springing from the two sources: the maintenance direct synergy, mainly indirect gregarious and position satisfactions, and the satisfactions in the group's work. The measurements and breakdowns of group attitudes into ergic vectors is an unexplored aspect of social psychology likely to have great power.

Returning to clinical aspects of motivation measurement, we have to see likewise in the near future an immense gain from the dynamic calculus: thereby the therapist will diagnose straightaway the field in which most of the inadequacy and conflict of an individual lie. This will be done from the magnitudes of the ten traits and the discrepancies of the U and I measures in each. Therapy will be followed up by noting intermittent changes on these traits by the periodic monitoring measures taken. A special four sub-test dynamic strength measure for the specific **symptom** of maladjustment need of the patient and comparing its change with changes on the underlying dynamic traits may need to be constructed. This was done by Birkett and Cattell (1978) in P-technique with a definite outcome in positive adjustment. New, quantitative laws of clinical and personality psychology remain to emerge from such practical studies in the dynamic calculus.

21   Some Points on Conflict, Learning, and Daily Decisions

In this chapter we propose to examine more closely a number of subtle points that have been left somewhat in the air in their first introductions above. First, we need more analysis of the distinction between arousal and activation. These have been found as definite factors in the Curran-Cattell Eight State Scale (1976) but not as yet in the handling of **specific** dynamic traits. We need evidence of the difference in loadings of these on specific ergic and semic factors and also evidence that the general states (in the C-C Battery) are in some sense summations of the activations or arousals of separate ergs or sems. (Actually in the C-C Battery the activation factor proves very similar in several loadings to the extroversion pattern. This suggests that various findings of Eysenck (1967) on extroversion need to be reexamined to see if they could be consequences of an activation **state**.) Parenthetically, we assume that arousal physiologically arises in the hypothalamus and that activation is a result of action on the reticular system.

Let us next turn to the measurement of conflict which have defined above as appearing in two forms: **active** and **indurated**. The latter has been shown to involve a loss of drive strength through some dynamic traits being positive and others negative in loading on an attitude action course. We have shown (Das, 1955; Williams, 1959) that indurated conflict and instability are correlated with ego weakness, and we see a three-cornered relation of ego strength in its absorption to a questionnaire factor, C, and to the MAT factors as shown by Cattell and Birkett (1980).

Finally, we have a measure of conflict in Sweney's clinical measurements (1964) which gives conflict a seven factor expression. The possibility that these seven factors represent frustrations on each of the seven motivation primaries has naturally been investigated by Krug (1971) and by Laughlin (1973), who checked the factors and found results compatible with each being an identity. It is certainly a theoretical simplification worthy of further study for we would then naturally have an index of conflict peculiar to each motivation primary, correlative to the $(U - I)$ index.

The role of active conflict in relation to everyday decisions has been examined by Laughlin (1973), who found a low positive agreement between the decision actually made in a life situation and the decision that would be predicted for the given person's trait strengths substituted in the behavioral equations (p. 130). It was also found that the individual's sense of a conflict was higher when the formula predicted it would be higher. However, tentative conclusions in this area presently rest on a maximum of one or two experiments so the whole question of fit of the model eagerly awaits experimenters.

Structured learning theory also awaits reinforcements, for its models are presently only partly supported by a handful of experiments. The theory that degree of engramming is predictable from the product of reverberation remnant and reward from tension reduction is hard to check by animal experiment because measures of reward size are confounded with initial deprivation size and the assignment of scores of different ergs is not possible as it is with the MAT in humans.

The equation for learning in humans is a complex one to handle experimentally. We have seen that it involves all the general personality traits, plus a reward effect, plus a CE effect as follows:

$$
\begin{aligned}
\text{Engram Gain} = {} & \Sigma b_{bjkx} T_{xi} + \Sigma b_{bjky} E_{yi} + \Sigma b_{bjkz} M_{zi} \\
& + \Sigma b_{bjkzy} M_{zi} E_{yi} + \Sigma b_{bjkyz} E_{yi} M_{zi} \\
& + \Sigma b_{jkr} (E_{t2i} - E_{t1i})/t_{2-1} + \Sigma b_{bjkt} hjkt_i
\end{aligned}
$$

$$(21\text{-}1)$$

Here the first five terms are the usual totality of ability-personality, T, and dynamic trait involvements, E and M, and the last two are, respectively, the reward effect and the effect from contiguity, CE, of stimuli—any instance of which is written $hjkt_i$. Leaving for the moment the general personality involvements, we recognize that

$$\Sigma b_{jkr} (E_{t2i} - E_{t1i})/t_{2-1} \qquad (21\text{-}2)$$

represents the duly weighted effect of the reward at its goal, $E_{t2i} - E_{t1i}$, divided by the time that has lapsed between the solving act and the solution (consummation). This needs to be added over all acts that contribute to the solution. The CE term which follows records the cognitive gains resulting from the insights or chance couplings of new stimuli with older ones already contributing to solution, e.g., recognition that a foreign word over a door means the same as enter.

Theoretically, the factoring of several learning gains, i.e., differences of two performances with constant external motivation (incentive) should yield all terms in Equation (21-1), but this would require extremely sensitive factor analysis and means of identification. Experimenters probably will prefer other approaches, controlling separately for the level of elements, e.g., taking the same group of subjects in two different reward conditions. Thus, we may answer such questions as whether the relation to t_{2-1} is linear or not and whether $E_{2i} - E_{1i}$ is better measured as a fall in arousal or primarily as a fall in need level as we believe.

Closer scrutiny is necessary in Equation (21-1) and others involving the simple motivation of an act, concerning what the E values stand for. We suppose that the first term, the **direct** stimulation of E by the environment (b_{hjky}), applies purely to the relevance of that environment to the **inherited** stimulability of the erg. It is, for example, not the real danger of a heavy truck in the street but the fearful noise it makes. An unfired revolver would have no such b_{hjky} since it has no innate meaning, and the arousal of fear derives purely from the activation of the acquired sentiment meaning, M_{zi}. Actually this M_{zi} value is a value that is specific to E_{xi} and would therefore require a term from the sem mandate (p. 37) expressing that particular stimulation value for E_{xi}. In Equation (21-1) we have considered that this is included in the weight, b_{hjkzy}, which includes the potency of the combination also in the learning act. To be thoroughly analytical we should have an extra weight in $b_{hjkzy}M_{zi}E_{xi}$ expressing the particular tie of M_z with E_x thus:

$$b_{hikzy} I_{zx} M_{zi} E_{xi} \tag{21-3}$$

in which I_{zx} is taken from the involvement vector showing the extent to which M_{zi} commands response from E_{xi}. These weights could be readily handled in a matrix statement of Equation (21-1).

It will be noted that by starting with b's as behavioral indices (loadings) we have avoided the complications in their breakdown to p, e, and s. p and e involve no complexity, but s, being connected with modulation, needs special discussion. It is a statement of how much the situation, k, arouses an erg or activates a sem, from past experience. It will be recognized that while p and e give the cognitive meaning of the situation, s gives its emotional, dynamic meaning, stressing the emotional liabilities that are involved thus:

$$S_{kxi} = x_{kx} L_{xi} \qquad (21\text{--}4)$$

formerly

(9–3)

where S_{kxi} is the state level to which liability to x is raised in i in situation k. (Incidentally, we recognize that in R-technique but not P-technique values this necessarily misses some of the individuality; because s_k is an average value for all people for the given situation, whereas i might have some more special value based on individual experience.) For most people the general emotional meaning of the situation k is the vector of k values across all emotional liabilities. The calculation of s_k values can be pursued in either of two ways (p. 49) and Cattell (1971, 1972), on which we need not further comment here.

The interesting possibility here is the objective grouping of social and other situations that is now possible by finding the similarity of their vectors, by applying the pattern similarity coefficient, r_p, to these profiles. From the matrix of r_p the Taxonome computer program will then group the situations into types from which a meaningful and practicable taxonomy of the emotional meaning of our chief cultural situations could be built up in social psychology.

Returning to the role of the behavioral equation in decisions, we encounter the problem of how a person spends time. So great a fraction of psychological experimentation is performed in laboratories where the person has agreed already to perform just the one task assigned that we know little about how a person decides to spend the day. Under comparatively free conditions the person is under the impact of a wide variety of stimulus situations, obligations, and inner appetitive conditions.

We know from experiments such as Shearer's (1984) that subjective appetitive and hormonal conditions help determine what comes into consciousness or action. As lunchtime approaches there are more images of food and thought about where to go for lunch. The prologue to a decision is therefore in part decided by ergic tension level that appears in the behavioral equation (p. 133, #21-3) as $E + EIM$. The rise in M may in turn stimulate the E's in the MIE terms. The next thing to do may therefore be decided by the attitude term most concerned with these E's and M's rising into consciousness. When it does so, it receives consideration by the ego, and perhaps the superego and self-sem, as well as by other attitudes competing from the basis of the risen ergs.

The behavioral equations are thus the directing forces in what a man does next, though the final decision depends on the weights of the controlling trio (C, G, and Q_3) as they examine the proposition. The decision thus depends on the internal stimuli, the external stimuli, and the coordinating powers operating in a decision among several attitude propositions. Unless the decision is a trivial one like going to the bathroom, the primary force usually will be the ego and it will exercise its function of stimulating images affecting those sems and ergs it needs for control by realistic evaluation of consequences.

The above analysis, of course, needs to be put to experiment to see if the decisions do in fact follow the combinations of meaning (b vector) and endowment (T vector) in each daily case of decision and spontaneous action.

22   Some Issues in the Principal Dynamic Calculus Equations

Since it may be questioned whether the reader yet has all the concepts in the dynamic calculus in a fully rounded perspective we propose to reexamine some key notions at some risk of repetition.

Structured learning theory, for example, departs from classical, Pavlovian-Skinnerian reflexology by

1. regarding the role of existing structures in learning
2. regarding the three mechanisms by which sentiment structures are built
3. listing three further learning principles and reanalyzing CR I as a combination of two of them
4. presenting a cognitive reverberation theory to account for reward, in connection with ergic tension reduction
5. proposing an equation to account for engram learning
6. describing learning as a complex change in *two* vectors, which acount for changes in ways of doing things
7. raising the probability that the quality of learning, e.g., its permanence, may be different for different ergs involved.

These seven points constitute a considerable difference and addition that call for extensive research.

The last is the only one we have perhaps not dealt with at all. It raises the question, for example, whether a skill or course of action learned under sex or hunger has the same wearing qualities as when learned under fear. There are at least indications that what is learned through security-seeking has a greater permanence, e.g., a greater resistance to clinical removal, than the same learned under a different erg.

Let us stop for a moment to recognize that most **skills** become available for use for *any* goal. We may have learned the rules of arithmetic under fear of a beating, but we can apply them to calculating when we shall next work out a holiday plan with our sweethearts. There is clearly a hierarchy of things learned, some of which can be readily disconnected from the original goal, while others are holons higher up in the emotional hierarchy that remain firm. For example, a man may fear for the safety of his country or his loved ones and be unable to shift the things he does for those ends to other ends; they belong there and nowhere else. Somewhere down the line from the top of the hierarchy of purposes down to the trivial skill or attachment, there is an increasing possibility of detachment. Indeed, we might say that one difference between a sem structure and an ability factor is that the latter can be used for any sem.

With this perspective we might consider some superego attitude, e.g., "Thou shalt not steal" built up under fear of parental loss of affection, with "Thou shalt be in time for lunch" built up partly under hunger. We know from animal experiment (Mackintosh, 1974) that a dynamic switch in learning generally causes a momentary marked loss of action, however, which is soon overcome. Let us suppose such effects are both past. We may well find, however, that stealing and coming late to lunch have very different resistances to change. The point is one of fundamental importance; it does suggest that in classical learning theory and experiments the use of the term conditioned, ignoring the ergic character of the reward, is missing something important.

The questions "What is an engram?" and "How is it retrieved?" remain. The systems theory (p. 94) supposes an immediate reference of any sensory presentation to a center P, which is the storage place of immediate memory powers. P also has exchanges, however, with the long-term memory of M and with the ergic storage, E, which interact mutually as well as with the controlling ego, D (Figure 16–2). The reaction to a stimulus thus means an immediate perceptual response, based on short-distance memory, and a longer term assimilation from the short-term storage to the whole long-term system in which encoding takes place. Here the immediate impression is broken down and sorted according to its reference parts into reference systems of recall (retrieval). It is lodged in the semic memory system, M, according to the sems to which it is most relevant; and if it is rewarded behavior, it is especially lodged in LM, subject to activation by ergic tensions.

When needed, the process of retrieval is by **association** in CE learning and by **purpose** in ME learning. But the purpose involves the action of cognative elements so M is prominant in both. Purpose involves **mental sets** to pick out what is wanted. Any motivation is a set, but a sem is a whole network of sets hierachially arranged beneath the main possessive mental set (attitude) to the sem object and concerned to preserve it. This connotes that every recall is aided by the main mental sets (attitudes in action) of sems and ergs too. The retrieval of an idea, e.g., of someone's street address, is therefore the work of all attitudes having to do with that person. This role of the attitudes is shown by the high loadings of information and fluency in the β and γ motivation components which constitute the I factor. The U component has not yet achieved these cognative contacts. In short, retrieval is a picking out by attitude action of perceptual and other cognative ideas that have been rearranged after perception in whatever systems the person uses but mainly by sentiments and some strictly logical categories.

The question remains unanswered as to whether continued availability of retrieval is partly dynamically maintained, i.e., whether continuing interest in a field is necessary for continuing engram storage. Several experiments suggest that committing an engram to memory does not insure its unchanging availability like storing an object in a museum. Quite apart from actual use of the idea its permanence is affected to some degree by the retention of the dynamic interest that committed it to memory. The Freudian unconscious we have suggested is maintained by an operation of making inaccessible the cognitive items that belong to the rebel dynamic trait concerned. The fading—if there is such—of an unused memory of low interest may well involve a lesser degree of the same phenomenon.

The proof and the design of proofing experiments in structured learning theory depend quantitatively upon the models in the dynamic calculus. This situation requires us to think carefully about the nature of the units with which we measure. In broad perspective there are two solutions to obtaining true zero measures: that deriving from **modulation theory** which simultaneously sets a true zero to a state and to the environmental stimulus causing it (Cattell, 1968; 1972; Cattell & Brennan, 1984) and that in the **relational simplex theory** of scaling by correlations (Cattell, 1962). These are presently only intermittently practicable. If we look at the 36 more important equations here as a final survey, the problem will stand out more readily.

Attitude strength simply, without M and E interaction:

$$a_{bijk} = b_{bjki}E_{1i} + \ldots + b_{bjkn}E_{ni} + b_{bjkm1}M_{1i} + b_{bjkmo}M_{oi} \qquad (5\text{--}1)$$

Attitude action with all traits operative:

$$a_{bijk} = \overset{x=b}{\underset{}{\Sigma}} b_{bjkx}A_{xi} + \overset{x=q}{\underset{}{\Sigma}} b_{bjky}P_{yi} + \overset{z=r}{\underset{}{\Sigma}} b_{bjkz}D_{zi} \qquad (5\text{--}2)$$

Ergic tension breakdown:

$$E_{xk} = (s_k + z) [x(C+H+I) + \{(P_k - aG_k) + (N_k - bG_s)\}] \qquad (6\text{--}1)$$

Active decision choice:

$$(a_{jiyk} - a_{bipk}) = (\overset{x=m}{\underset{}{\Sigma}} b_{bjkx}E_{xi} + \overset{y=n}{\underset{}{\Sigma}} b_{bjky}M_{yi}) - (\overset{x=m}{\underset{}{\Sigma}} b_{bpk}E_{xi}$$
$$+ \overset{y=n}{\underset{}{\Sigma}} b_{bpk}M_{yi}) \qquad (7\text{--}1)$$

Conflict in active decision:

$$C_{bjckp} = \frac{a_{bijk} + a_{bipk}}{a_{bijk} - a_{bipk}} \qquad (7\text{--}2)$$

Conflict in indurated conflict:

$$C_{bjk} = \frac{\Sigma \bar{b}_{bjk}}{\Sigma \bar{b}_{bjk} + \Sigma \overset{+}{b}_{bjk}} \qquad (7\text{--}3)$$

Integration:

$$I = \Sigma \frac{1}{c} \qquad (7\text{--}4)$$

Control of adverse impulse:

$$a_{bijk} = \overset{x=p}{\underset{}{\Sigma}} b_{bijkx}E_{xi} + \overset{y=q}{\underset{}{\Sigma}} b_{bjky}M_{yi} - b_{bjk}C_{ci} - b_{bjkg}G_{gi} - b_{bjkq}Q_{c3i}$$
$$(8\text{--}1)$$

Path Learning Analysis, *PLA*:

$$L_p \times E = B \qquad (9\text{--}2)$$

Determiner Potency Analysis:

$$PDLE = T \tag{9-3}$$

Solution for potencies for given traits:

$$P_{d1} = L_{d1} D_{d1} (D_{d1} D'_{d1})^{-1} \tag{9-5}$$

$$S_{xik} = s_{kx} L_{xi} \tag{10-1}$$

Relation of factorial indices:

$$b = (p + e)s \tag{10-4a} \tag{12-3}$$

Prediction with regard to effect of particular ideas:

$$a_{bijk} = \Sigma b_{bijkx} A_{xi} + \Sigma b_{biky} P_{yi} + \Sigma b_{bjkz} D_{zi} + b_{bjkp} I_{pi}$$
$$+ b_{bjkq} I_{qi} \tag{10-5}$$

Anxiety level from uncertainty:

$$a_{ei} = (f)(E_{xi} + M_{yi} E_{xi}) V_d (E_{fi} - H_i) \tag{11-1}$$

Anxiety level from ego control threat:

$$a_{ci} = (f) \frac{(E_{xi} + M_{yi} E_{xi})}{(C + Q_3) - V(E_{xi} + M_{yi} E_{xc})} \tag{11-2}$$

Anxiety level from amount of frustration:

$$a_{pi} = (f)(E_{xi} + M_{yi} E_{xi}) - E_{xri} \tag{11-3}$$

Total anxiety:

$$A_{xi} = a_{ei} + a_{ci} + a_{pi} \tag{11-4}$$

Relation of environmentally produced change to specific environmental variance:

$$r_{e_x t_y} = \frac{r_{e_x (g+t)y}}{r_{ty(g+t)y}} \tag{12-1}$$

Same relation, different source:

$$r^2_{ty(g+t)y} = 1 - H \tag{12-2}$$

Engramming as a function of reward and time:

$$\eta = (a_{j2} - a_{j1}) = E_R\,m/t \tag{13-1}$$

Learning as a function of structure and reward:

$$\eta = \Sigma v_a s_a A + \Sigma v_p s_p P + \Sigma v_d s_d D + E_R\,m/t \tag{13-2}$$

Assumed value of reward effect:

$$E_R\,m/t = N\cdot E_R\,(vs_{ke}E + vs_{km}ME + v_{skm}M)/t \tag{13-3}$$

Multi-id sources of variance in person-centered model:

$$a_{bijko} = \Sigma b_{jx}T_{xi} + \Sigma b_{by}T_{yi} + \Sigma b_{kz}T_{zi} + \Sigma b_{op}T_{pi} \tag{14-1}$$

Additive mode of total behavioral sources (three ids):

$$a_{ij} + a_{jk} + a_{ik} = \Sigma b_{jx}T_x + \Sigma w_{ky}P_{yi} + \Sigma y_{iz}Q_{xk} \tag{14-2}$$

Relation of individual to cultural element:

$$\begin{array}{cccc} P & \times & C & = & I \\ (N \times u) & (u \times u) & (N \times u) \end{array} \tag{14-3}$$

Bridging equation econetics to dynamics:

$$\begin{array}{cccc} I & \times & E & = & G \\ (N \times u) & (u \times z) & (N \times z) \end{array} \tag{14-4}$$

Individualized econetic-dynamic outcome:

$$\begin{array}{cccc} G & : & D & = & Q \\ (N \times z) & (N \times z) & (N + z) \end{array} \tag{14-5}$$

General econetic formula:

$$(P \times C \times E) \cdot D = Q \tag{14-6}$$

Ego is modified by CEP action and other traits:

$$C = (b_{ca}A + b_{cb}B + b_{cc}C + b_{cd}D + \ldots) \tag{15-1}$$

Introduction of E and M interaction in behavior:

$$a_{bijk} = \overset{x=b}{\sum} b_{bjkx} E_{xi} + \overset{y=biq}{\sum} b_{bjk} \times eyE_{xi}M_{yi} + \overset{y=q}{\sum} b_{bjky}M_{yi} \qquad (16\text{-}2)$$

Syntality from population and structure:

$$S = (f)PC \qquad (17\text{-}2)$$

Operation of the full motivation components in an attitude:

$$a_{bijk} = bE' + bE'' + s_{ke}E_1 + s_{km}ME + S_kM + (s_{km}M - M)$$
$$+ (s_{ke}EM - M) \qquad (18\text{-}1)$$

Attitude motivation in motivation components:

$$a_{bijk(d)} = b_{bjkg}E'_i + b_{bjke}E''_i + b_{bjkg}E_i + b_{bjkg}E_{2i} \qquad (19\text{-}1)$$

School grades by motivation:

$$\text{Ach} = 0.44SE - 0.23SA + 0.37SS - 0.15 \text{ Sex} - 0.24 \text{ Fear}$$
$$+ 0.21 \text{ Pugnac.} - 0.33 \text{ Narc.} + 0.36 \text{ Construct.} \qquad (20\text{-}1)$$

All sources gain in engram learning:

$$\text{Gain} = \Sigma b_{bjkx}T_{xi} + \Sigma b_{bjky}E_{yi} + \Sigma b_{bjkz}M_{zi} + \Sigma b_{bjkzy}M_{zi}E_{yi}$$
$$+ \Sigma b_{bjkyz}E_{yi}M_{zi} + \Sigma b_{bjkr}(E_{t2i} - E_{t1i})/t_{2-1} + \Sigma b_{bjkt}bjkt_i$$
$$(21\text{-}1)$$

Introduction of ergic involvement, I, into learning term:

$$b_{jjkzy}I_{zx}M_{zi}E_{yi} \qquad (21\text{-}3)$$

These 37 equations express the main propositions in the dynamic calculus as it has stood to this time. In virtually all cases the units of measurement are typically standard scores on personality factors while the same is true of the actual dependent behaviors, and the b's range from -1.0 to 1.0. Most of the equations ignore specific factors which are in factor analysis, generally unrecognized as unlocated general factors, though in some highly specific a's they may be truly specific entities. In that case their roles can only become evident as behavior unaccounted for by the broad personality factors, i.e., the part of a unpredicted by our general broad factor analysis. Probably specific factors are most frequent in the dynamic field due to quite specific conditioning of a very narrow "interest behavior."

The other deviation here from the usual behavioral equations, Equation (10-5), is the importation of terms for the intrusion of particular ideas, memories, and concepts affecting the response (I's in the equation). These might be considered outlying fragments of common, broad sentiments and thus be included in M; but frequently these represent ideas, even skills that have long ceased to be attached to particular sems though they need to be accounted for by being shepherded in, under the influence of one or more sems.

There is an untouched problem here for unitary trait theory. How does it happen that when the main sem is evoked, for example, to my wife, who is out with a car breakdown, that I think of a particular station to which she can go and that I phone that station? Under the drive of the sem to my wife I not only experience the rise of various attitudes to her such as her impractical nature but lead on to the solution of calling station X? Reasoning with images has played a major part until I reach station X as the means of helping her. Calling X involves not only the wife sentiment, the erg of protectiveness, the superego, and other broad traits, but also a recollection of X having specifically been helpful before. Specific behaviors are thus full of specific ideas and recollections additional to the main ergs and sems. First, they enter from a mental experiment, commonly with verbal and nonverbal imagery, in which means to satisfaction of sems or ergs are brought into active play. Second, they may arise as the products of earlier CE action in which contiguity recalls them. Whichever way these particular concepts appear, they can be noteworthy aids to a particular action and need to be incorporated in the behavioral equation as we finally represent it in Equation (10-5) above. The score that goes in for these special adjuncts ranges as a standard score from -2.5 to $+2.5$, with a b value that can be experimentally found. Probably these special adjuncts, by reason of their dependence on individual history, will be detected first in P-technique experiments. Our alcoholic (Birkett & Cattell, 1978) saw an image of a particular brand of whisky in times of high rise in his alcoholic symptom (sem), which affected his P-technique score seemingly appreciably and could be detected as an extra sem in factoring. From loadings on massive sems to loadings on quite specific concepts the bridge in behavioral equations is one which now needs to enter the model and to be explored by particularly sensitive factor analyses. It is one of the major points of exchange of classical reflexology and the dynamic calculus.

There are, of course, some hypothetical statements in the above equations that call for fuller discussion. In the first place the construction of Equation (6-1) involves a common-sense breakdown of need strength into appetitive and nonappetitive parts and of appetitive into behavior appetitive and physiological consummation appetitive. These breakdowns are evident in experiment and seem reasonable.

The three sources of anxiety have been propounded for some time (Spielberger, 1973). No experiment has yet checked them directly though they hold in general clinical observation.

What is of central importance in the dynamic calculus in relation to learning is set out in Equations (12-1) through (13-3). These equations need closest examination and carefully planned experiments if structured learning theory is to offer the advances we believe it contains. Equations (14-1) through (14-6) offer broader means of obtaining perspective on the main influences in determining a response and in the econetic model of making a new calculation in social psychology from which valuable laws could well emerge. The remaining equations lead us into the new ideas of structured learning theory and entertain the hypothesis about the mystery of seven primary motivation components, still insufficiently investigated.

23   Some Speculative Advances

With the framework of experimentally tolerably supported concepts reached to this point, let us now more freely enter on some speculative hypotheses. The first question is whether each individual has a sum total of ergic energy on which the systems theory model draws. This could appear as a general factor in the correlation of ergs, but the question, complicated by ipsative scoring, has never yet been properly investigated. We assume there must be some limit to each erg and to all ergs to account for stimulation not leading to a runaway positive feedback.

A second question of general relevance concerns the power of subgoals to remain active **after** they cease to subsidiate to ergic goals. We see apparent action of this kind in a number of sentiments such as the superego which first subsidiated to the present and was held by the threat of loss of parental affection but which still remains powerfully active in later life. It is apparent also in Allport's (1938) perception of functional autonomy in which he believed that after a length of time a subgoal became sufficient in itself to maintain action. We have surmised that this really does not occur **absolutely** because it would beget the pursuit of many behaviors that lead nowhere with change of situation. Yet, we must grant that much human behavior is so slow to change that it seems the power invested in the subgoal **tends** to remain. The alternative explanation to sheer persistence is that in the course of complex human learning subgoals for ergic satisfaction, x, become used also, in part, as means of ergic goal, Y, which causes the subgoal to retain potency with X otherwise satisfied. Thus, it could happen that the superego behavior, directed at first to pleasing the parent, becomes directed to what the older child recognizes as fair and just behavior to others like himself (as Piaget argues). In this case the superego injunctions should lose some of the terror that guided them in the infant and his identification (Freudian) with the father. There is no quantitative evidence of this though there is a growth and switch in the nature of the prohibitions (Kohlberg, 1973; Cattell & Carter, 1985) compatible with this. Subgoals evidently lose their cue power very slowly.

The role of subgoals has other puzzling properties. The reaching of a subgoal apparently gives a relief (reward) of ergic tension while at the same time a fresh stimulating arousal and expectation of the goal. The person flying from Los Angeles to New York on an uncertain reservation is happy when he reaches Chicago, but is not his desire to complete his journey further aroused by getting so far? Present-day measurement of ergic tension and sem activation levels by tests like the MAT and SMAT theoretically puts us at last in a position to measure ergic tension levels at subgoals and to plot the curves in Figure 23-1, but the length of time needed for a measurement is such that experimentation is impracticable except in very specially planned experiments not yet done. The vital issue of the discharging and recharging effects of reaching subgoals therefore remains unanswered in humans along with the answer to the question on p. 77 of what weight should be given to the drop in arousal as well as in need strength in their contribution to learning.

Many psychologists will also have some doubts about alignment of the seven factors in conflict manifestations with the frustrations of the seven motivation component primaries since direct proof has not yet been supplied. Conflict factor VI, for example, with its increased pugnacity and anxiety over the choice and its vacillation over decisions, suggests an anxiety begotten of frustration of the ego motivation factor, β, while V with its hope for a guessed success and its uneven sensitivity to insults might be the superego factor, γ. These are matchings that could be pursued by factorings carrying vital variables for both, applied to the same laws of conflict.

In general, it can be said that the dynamic calculus with its precise models and its foundation in measurement contains altogether firmer hope of experimental progress than most dynamic theories. Madsen (1968; 1974) in his intensive survey of 24 dynamic theories (McDougall, Maslow, Pribram, Berlyne, Hebb, Hall, Tolman, and others) places the dynamic calculus at the top in terms of the HQ (Hypothesis/fact Quotient) for **testability**. This careful evaluation promises the greatest progress in its propositions, though ingenuity of plans is going to be needed in measurement. For example, the various comparisons needed of the size of U and I components in ergs and sems in recent and older attitudes and in conflict measure require that despite different contents the U and I measures shall be quantitatively comparable.

A considerable problem in human learning research is that in daily

TABLE 23-1.   Age Curves for Dynamic Structure Traits

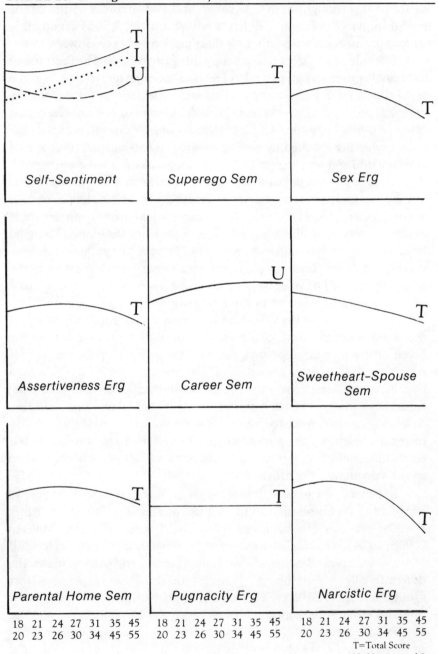

18	21	24	27	31	35	45
20	23	26	30	34	45	55

18	21	24	27	31	35	45
20	23	26	30	34	45	55

18	21	24	27	31	35	45
20	23	26	30	34	45	55

T=Total Score
U=Unintegrated Score
I=Integrated Score

(Based on 220 cases measured by Michael Anton on the MAT.)

It will be noted that the two are also measured elsewhere (Cattell 1973) by the 16 PF show identical age change on the two devices life our learnings in different paths go on simultaneously. A person is learning to typewrite, to sail a boat, to study medicine, and to experience personality factor changes in interactions with people, all at the same time. We switch from one activity to another throughout the day according to the demands of circumstances. How does the experimenter connect the rewards (the changes in ergic tension) with progress in learning medicine, for example, when the measured tension levels are simultaneously begotten by other paths? By taking tension levels hourly and daily on all ergs and recording the phase in each path hourly, the experimenter may build up a series of simultaneous equations, each giving a tension measure for a given combination of path events. By solving these equations so much of the tension can be apportioned to each. For example, let us suppose measures on three days over which concern about medical exams goes up 1, 2, and 3, while that on learning to type stays steady, and that concerning attraction to a girl is reported falling by 4, 3, and 2, then three MAT measures on self assertion might be 12, 6, and 8.

$$1. \quad 12 = 1M + 2T + 4G$$
$$2. \quad 16 = 2M + 2T + 3G$$
$$3. \quad 8 = 3M + 2T + 2G$$

Then from (1) and (2) we have $4 = M$ and from (2) and (3) $8 = 1M + 2G$ when $G = 6$, and so $T = 8$. These are the strengths of three dynamic traits, which can be translated to state levels per day and related to learning gains in the given paths. It does require an evaluation by ulterior means of the rises and declines of separate interests which could be by self-evaluation or special sem measurements.

This raises the question whether single measurements can be set up that measure not merely the total strength of a sem, which we know we can do, but the strength of a particular erg in a particular sem, for example, the amount of self-assertion achieving satisfaction through a sentiment to mastering typewriting or computer work in a given individual. Normally we would get an estimate of this through a group factor analysis showing the regression of self-assertion on the sentiment and estimating the former from the sem score. Although such tests have not yet been devised, it shoud be possible to present stimuli for the sentiment which deliberately involve the self-assertive component in its action. For example, "I like to typewrite because I gain satisfaction of a sense of mastery" presented through the usual projection, autism, etc. devices would seem to meet this need for an individual's score.

Immediately analytic measures as we may call such estimates of a given erg in a given sentiment in a given individual would be very valuable clinically. The MAT gives total ergic tensions (U and I) and total sentiment strengths; but as evidence of what erg is involved in what sentiment, we have only the **common** b weights which may be wide of the mark for a particular clinical case. The design of immediately analytic measures binding the measure of the erg to a particular sentiment calls for a feat in test design that few may be capable of executing. In principle it should be possible by locating the sem activities that lead to a particular ergic goal to design the motivation component devices around those activities. Since the number of combinations of ergs with sems is quite great, such construction is likely to be undertaken only for an important minority, e.g., the ergs in the self sem, in the occupation and in the home. These connections are important guides to therapeutic steps.

In evaluating the normality of developmental level in a sem we naturally take the sex, age, and cultural setting of the individual into account. The sex differences can be considerable. On the MAT men are significantly higher on pugnacity and career interest and women on superego and self-sentiment (Cattell, Radcliffe, and Sweney, 1963). This is on U measures for on I measures differences arise only in higher male fear and pugnacity and higher female narcism, sweetheart, and home attachment.

On age there is a rise through the developmental years on fear, narcism, and self sem and a fall in parental home attachment for joint male/female scores. A matter of structural interest is the correlation of self-sentiment and superego measured by MAT and by questionnaire. Factors with the same meaning clearly emerge in both media, but although the correlations are higher between them than any other correlations they are not really high: 0.38 for SS and 0.21 for G. Corrected for attenuation these could rise to identity levels, yet there remains an interesting difference due to the media, objective test versus questionnaire. We can see that the questionnaire deals with the individual's conscious awareness of interests in self-image (in the self sem) whereas the objective test gets more at the total conscious and unconscious interest. Nevertheless, the appearance of the same factors in the two media is proof of the reality of structures independently of the media of observation (the **indifference of indicator** principle).

In accordance with our belief that a psychological system **initially** should depend entirely on behavioral evidence we have not made reference to physiology and anatomy in the neural field up to this point;

but the concepts we have developed have relationships to the reticular formation, the cortex, the forebrain, the hypothalamus, the hippocampus, the septum, the amygdala, the lingulum, and much else now fairly well investigated neurally. We see systematic connections of psychological concepts with these in the work of Pribram, Hebb, Eysenck, and others. Our approach is a descriptive parallelism to the motivational structure and action. The hypothalamus is the home of ergic arousal as the reticular formation is the seat of activation. (Note Eysenck has switched around our distinctive operational use of activation and arousal.) The cognitive controls on the hypothalamus reside in the general cognitive associations of sems in the cortex. In particular, the frontal lobes with their projections on the hypothalamus are expectedly the seat of C, G, and Q_3 as inhibitory forces. The interactions of activation and arousal operate through the flow between the hypothalamus and the reticular system. This is as far as we can go at present, though such theories as those of Hebb, Miller, Eysenck, Young, and others bring some speculative surplus meaning out of physiology into psychology. As yet no precise work with our measurements—except perhaps that of Royce and Covington (1960)—has explained physiological relationships so we remain at speculation.

It goes without saying that we see all psychological and physiological action as hierarchical, couched in a succesion of semiautonomous action centers which Koestler (1967) calls holons. Thus, many simple reflex matters are adequately handled at the spinal level with possible intervention from higher holons if needed. Typewriting, driving a car, carrying on a simple conversation also look after themselves up to a point, but higher levels of conscious control enter when difficulties are met. Neurological damage mainly interferes with the rote memory involved in the lower activities and leaves the consciousness of self unimpaired, though there is often therewith a reduction of fluid and crystallized intelligence. This integration of hierarchies is what reflexology (behaviorism) fails to incorporate. It means that the whole is more than a sum of parts from the bottom row as structured learning theory makes clear. Neurologically the control in a hierearchy from above downwards is more evident than in behavioral structure, though we have made it clear that the role of the ego is as a **supreme** integrator.

24

Problems for
Further Investigation

Just as chemistry became a science with the quantitative, mathematical experiments of Lavoisier and Dalton so may we reasonably hope that human motivation will do so with the advent of the dynamic calculus.

There is much to be done, and the present chapter will devote itself to raising the appropriate questions in research. There are obvious tasks like extending knowledge of the number and nature of ergs in our race and sems in our culture. These are full of fascinating subquestions concerning the naturalistic b values of everyday situations on innate ergic tendencies and on the manner of rise of sems. There are more subtle model questions as raised in Madsen's fine philosophical treatment of modern motivation theories (1974), for example. Let us consider these growing points in the field.

Incidentally, it should be recognized that in a stabilized attitude the s_k terms represent the individual's degree and kind of **satisfaction** from the course of action.

A matter of considerable importance concerns the model of interaction of ergs and sems which we have stated in Equations (21–1) and (16–2) above, namely:

$$a_{hijk} = \overset{x=m}{\underset{}{\Sigma}} b_{hjkx} E_{xi} + \overset{x=m}{\underset{}{\Sigma}}\overset{y=n}{\underset{}{\Sigma}} b_{hjkxy} E_{xi} M_{yi}$$

$$+ \overset{y=n}{\underset{}{\Sigma}}\overset{x=m}{\underset{}{\Sigma}} b_{hjkyx} M_{yi} E_{xi} + \overset{y=n}{\underset{}{\Sigma}} b_{hjky} M_{yi} \qquad (21\text{–}1)$$

We have agreed that factor analysis so far has yielded clearly only the first and last of these terms; but we know that it frequently treats products as if they were sums when investigated in the additive, linear model, and we are venturing to assume that this is what happens here. After all, the two middle terms are quite complex, each being representable in matrix terms as the product of several matrices, as shown in Figure 24–1. The first matrix on the left simply has the involvement of each sem, recorded as many times in the column as there are ergs, m. The second is the individual/endowment matrix for each individual in all sems. The result of multiplying these we use as the total semic endowment in each erg which represents the **involvement-by-semic strength**. This matrix, removed to Figure 24–2, is then multiplied by the actual strength of the erg to give a final diagonal matrix representing the total involvement of each of n sems in the totality of m ergs for each individual. These dynamic values are finally multiplied by b to give the impact of the ergic-semic interaction on the behavior. This should be represented by a final matrix multiplication of b values and an identity matrix if we assume, surely as we may have to, that each ergic-semic interaction has its own weight. The last matrix on the right is thus multiplied by an identity vector to sum to a single value for the EM contribution. It is evident that no fewer than n different ergic products enter the final EM summed effect.

The argument for the ME term is just the same as for the EM term in Equation (24–1), ending in m product effects, representing the result of each E being aroused by n sentiments. That is to say, both EM and ME terms need similar matrix calculation. Since a_{hijk} is covered by all motivation primaries, the score includes the effect of the product terms plus the pure ergic innate contribution and the pure acquired M contribution presumably to the β and γ terms (I factor). We now observe Equation (24–1) should include a matrix term for the involvement of each erg in each sem (second term in 24–2) and, conversely, of each sem activating each erg. This is necessary because the stimulating action of M on E (and vice-versa) will surely depend on the natural degree of involvement between the two. The discovery of the involvement values can be made as suggested earlier (p. 129). Therefore, to use Equation (24–1) we need only the behavioral indices which can be obtained from correlations of the trait and trait combinations measures with a_{hijk}.

The fecundity of the dynamic calculus is evident especially in the area of conflict where several promising theories need to be brought to a common experimental check (7–2 and 7–4b above). These concern the assessment of total conflict by the P-technique indurated conflict index and relating it to ego strength, C, the amount of instability of attitudes

144

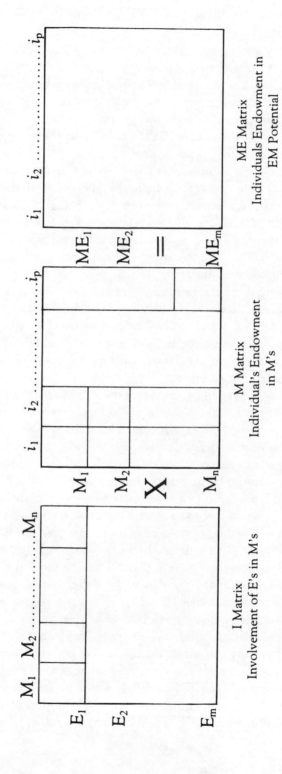

FIGURE 24-1. Calculation of individual's *ME* potential by matrices.

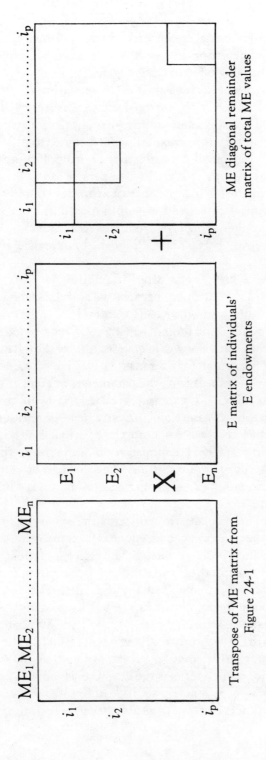

FIGURE 24–2. Calculation of individuals actual *ME* contribution by matrices.

145

over time, the dynamic disagreement (cognitive dissonance) of attitudes, and the degree of development of defense mechanisms. They should correlate as from a single factor, the C factor.

Decision theory needs investigation by seeing how far the b's from R-technique, combined with personal trait measures, will predict a person's practical decisions and finding what improvement comes from using P-technique b's. Here also experiments designed to produce higher activation in relevant, loaded sentiments or arousal in ergs could be tested in connection with a psychology of persuasion or brainwashing. For knowledge of the b's in a number of attitudes should show most clearly where arousal or activation would most influence a decision. This approach applies equally, of course, to removing a particular symptom in therapy, where b's and T's are the basic articles on which to operate.

At present we know relatively little about the usual course of arousal and subsidence of an erg because we have lacked measures for specific ergic tensions, until the MAT. Central here is the question of a natural limit to arousal, of the borrowing of energy by one erg from another, and of the relative power in engramming of the fall measured at consummation in arousal (ergic tension) relative to need strength. There is also scope for measuring the parameters of ergic goal consummatory behaviors. What, for example, are the specific life characters of reward behavior for self-assertion, curiosity, fear, gregariousness, and other nonviscerogenic ergs? An example of what is needed here is Harlow and Harlow's (1965) demonstration of the role in the parental (and the appeal) ergs of tactile softness. The b weight of a situation on the innate part (Equation (24–1)) of ergic stimulation is what needs to be tied down here.

A domain of some obscurity concerns the extent to which **satisfaction** in a course of action can be equated with the value of the ergic and semic modulation indices, the s_k's. The concept of the s_k is that it is a measure differing from the p and e indices of the extent to which the situation k excites a particular, usually dynamic, trait. This level of activation or arousal must indicate how much the situation natively or by previous experience has satisfied the given drive. We assume that the provocation of a drive without satisfying it will result in a falling to zero of s_k. Thus, **temporarily** s_k may have a value other than the satisfaction value, but in the long run it reflects the extent to which the situation has led to satisfaction—or is innately set to lead to satisfaction. It is what Hull (1952) and others referred to as the retroactive reinforcer subgoal in a stream of subgoals representing leading to satisfactions in earlier runs. It seems reasonable, therefore, to equate the s_k's with the satisfaction commonly achieved by the course of action concerned in a stable history of learning. In a straight line tract in the lattice with no runoffs we should expect that the s_k's would be the same at all points, barring attrition. However, since there *is* attrition in that the maze animal, for example, does not always run to the end, experiments may show that the s_k's nearer the goal are higher. Meanwhile, however, we conclude that the sum of s_k's in a behavioral equation represents the total satisfaction in that course.

Another dynamic calculus implication that may not be obvious concerns the almost constant change that must go on in the lattice through the appetitive instability of the ergic needs. For example, a man in a high state of hunger or sex will, acording to our P-technique experiments, experience a rise in all the numerous attitudes that subsidiate to these ergic goals. This will produce fairly wide changes in the s_k's of subsidiating attitude chains affecting the strengths of sentiments generally. There resides in the self-sentiment and the ego the means to correct these switches in the interest of long-term satisfaction. The hungry man does not devour everything in the kitchen refrigerator when he reflects that no one will replace things that day. The extent of control of appetitive swings would depend here on the sentiment to home as well as the general controllers, but stability of attitudes is, in general, a function of C.

A development of the dynamic calculus that reaches the heart of everyday behavior is in the realization that every sem is both a structure and a process. The process, which we investigated on p. 125, expresses a coordination of the modulating influences, s_k's, internally and externally evoked with the effects of specific stimuli, h's, encountered at possible choice points. The initial s_k evoking and activating the whole sentiment is what keeps behaviors true to the main sem purpose. If at some point a larger s_k occurs to divert behavior to another sem, the behavior will start off on another track; but normally it will "persist with varied effort," the varied effort being responsive to the strengths of the specific stimuli that are encountered. These specific stimuli are both h's, determining the immediate course of action response, and k's, enhancing the basic s_k of the sem.

Only by this process model of the sem can we account for the flow of everyday behavior. At this point we must inspect more closely the inner sources which we have always supposed to operate with external stimulus situations in s_k's. The s_k that is operative in a new situation often clearly contains some value from preceding events as in a man who decides on a new plan in his office while he is still under the influence of an enraging previous frustration. States obviously enter into s_k's which thus cease to be merely expressions of an external situation, k. Past events thought of by the individual help determine its magnitude. This must be recognized by having the model include several contributing s_k's in any final s_k. Accordingly, we should really write in the behavioral equation,

$$v_{hjk} s_k T = v_{hjk} (s_{k1} + s_{k2} \ldots s_{kn}) T \qquad (24\text{-}2)$$

where the s_k's enter from a variety of past experiences. The magnitude of these s_k's perhaps might be obtained from determining the b's for the given sem in various behaviors and treating the total s_k in each case as the basis of a simultaneous equation.

The determination of s_k values is in any case a central undertaking for cognitive and dynamic psychology. These values explain the meaning of life situations and are the basis of conflict estimation. It is possible that the action of the ego is best understood as a stimulator of appropriate sems and ergs as we have conjectured. In that framework we see it as operating on s_k's thus (see also Equation 15-1):

$$a_{hij} = v_{hjkx} (s_{kx} s_{hxc}) M_x + \ldots v_{hjky} (s_{ky} + s_{kyc}) M_y \qquad (24\text{-}3)$$

Here s_{kx} and s_{ky} are the normal activation values of k for the sems x and y; but s_{kxc} and s_{kyc} are direct stimulating influences of the ego control factor, C, upon them. Factorially this would lead to C appearing as a second order factor among sentiments, **if many a_{hjk}'s could be found where it acts on sems similarly**. At present there is no evidence of C acting among sems other than as another primary factor, but it is not yet thoroughly investigated and it seems psychologically probable that it operates in decisions by modulating the action of sems by recalling their successful roles in previous situations. The s_k's are clearly the main coinage in the interaction of sems, and new laws may well be found when we determine the values of that coinage in many situations, sems, and ergs.

Very little research has been directed to developmental aspects of human motivation in dynamic calculus terms. We have some brief age range data on levels of dynamic traits (Figure 23-1, p. 138). There is nothing as yet on the growth of **form** of sentiments checking on the three bases of their origin as unitary traits except for the superego. As regards the role of genetics we have two possibilities to consider:

1. sentiment forms entirely threptic (formed from environment) will have no more than a chance relation of outline to the genetic, ergic pattern nearest to it, and

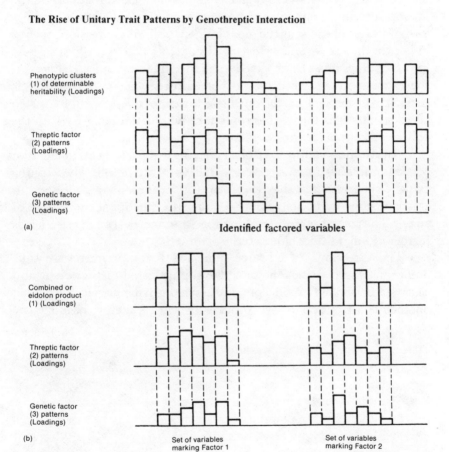

The Rise of Unitary Trait Patterns by Genothreptic Interaction

Phenotypic clusters
(1) of determinable
heritability (Loadings)

Threptic factor
(2) patterns
(Loadings)

Genetic factor
(3) patterns
(Loadings)

(a)

Identified factored variables

Combined or
eidolon product
(1) (Loadings)

Threptic factor
(2) patterns
(Loadings)

Genetic factor
(3) patterns
(Loadings)

(b)

Set of variables
marking Factor 1

Set of variables
marking Factor 2

Two models of possible genothreptic interaction in producing observed unitary phenotypic structures: (a) amalgamated model (in divisive basis): factor overlap of distinct genetic and threptic patterns; (b) the box-and-lid or eidolon model of overlap of factor patterns. The top row is in each case the sum of the two below.

FIGURE 24-3. Two genothreptic possibilities in sem development.

2. the eidolon (box-and-lid) model that supposes threptic influences to concentrate their effects around the original genetic form as shown in Figure 24–3.

In the anthropology of the rise of social institutions we see signs of building up institutions partly **around** the expression of particular ergs, e.g., sex and of fear, and alternatively, partly in complex response ((a) in Figure 24.3) to the needs of some subsociety. The pattern of loaded attitudes for an erg typically shows its highest loadings on the most direct and final, consummatory expression. The lower loadings are of interest in showing the more hidden, oblique expressions such as music for the sex erg and wish for self-control in the case of fear. These lower loadings must be expected to be specific to a culture, delineating the expressions of the drive in that culture. The score on an ergic tension will depend partly on those lower loading contributions so although an erg is innate its expressions will, of course, vary with the culture, except in its consummation.

An area now calling for study concerns the extent of fragmentation of sems, notably as they rise and fall with activation. The existing evidence suggests that they rise from fragmentations in childhood to greater unity in adult life, seldom reaching the functional unitarinism of an erg. The role of sems in evoking specific concepts (p. 58) also needs further *dR*- and *P*-technique study.

The directions of advance indicated for experiment are thus numerous and diverse. They involve sophisticated methodology and clear perception of the conceptual issues in the dynamic calculus model, but their contribution to psychology as a science is likely to be immense.

Bibliography

Adelson, M. A study of ergic tension patterns through the effects of water deprivation in humans. Unpublished Ph.D. dissertation, University of Illinois, Urbana, 1952.

Allport, G.W., *Personality: A Psychological interpretation.* New York: Holt, 1938.

Anton, M. The construction of the B form of the MAT. Ph.D. Dissertation, Hawaii School of Professional Psychology, Honolulu, 1985.

Bandura, A. Social learning through imitation. In Jones, M.R. (Ed.) *Nebraska Symposium on Motivation.* Lincoln: University of Nebraska Press, 1962.

Barton, K. & Cattell, R.B. Personality before and after a chronic illness. *J. of Clinical Psychology,* 1972a, 28, 464–467.

Barton, K. & Cattell, R.B. Personality factors related to job promotion and turnover. *J. of Counselling Psychology,* 1972b, 19, 430–435.

Bartsch, J. Personal Communication on Research Results, 1973.

Berlyne, D.E. *Conflict, Arousal and Curiosity.* New York: McGraw-Hill, 1960.

Bertalanphy, L. von, *General systems theory: Foundations, developments, application.* New York: Braziller, 1969.

Birkett, H. & Cattell, R.B. Diagnosis of the dynamic roots of a clinical symptom by P-technique. A case of episodic alcoholism. *Multivariate Experimental Clinical Research,* 1978, 3, 173–194.

Blodgett, H.C. The effect of introduction of reward upon the maze performance of rats. *Publications in Psychology,* University of California, 1929, 4, 113–134.

Boyle, G.J. Effects on academic learning of manifestating emotional states and motivational dynamics. *British J. of Educational Psychology,* 1983, 53, 347–357.

Brennan, J. & Cattell, R.B. A comparison of factoring ipsatized and unipsatized scores. (in press) 1984.

Burt, C. L. *The Young Delinquent.* London: University of London Press, 1927.

Cannon, W.B. *The Wisdom of the Body.* London: Norton, 1932.

Cattell, Heather, The art of combining tests, biography, & interview in clinical psychotherapy. In Cattell, R.B. & Johnson, R. (Eds.) *Functional Psychological Testing.* New York: Brunner Mazel, 1984.

Cattell, R.B. The concept of social status. *J. of Social Psychology,* 1942, 15, 293–308.

———. Fluctuation of sentiments and attitudes as a measure of character integration and of temperament. *American J. of Psychology*, 1943, 56, 195–216.

———. *The Description and Measurement of Personality*. New York: World Book, 1946.

———. On the theory of group learning, *J. Social Psychology*, 1953, 37, 27–52.

———. The dynamic calculus: a system of concepts derived from objective motivation measurements. In G. Lindzey (Ed.) *The Assessment of Human Motive*. New York: Rinehart, 1958.

———. The dynamic calculus: Concepts and crucial experiments. In M.R. Jones (Ed.) *The Nebraska Symposium on Motivation* Lincoln: University of Nebraska Press, 1959.

———. The relational simplex theory of equal internal & absolute scaling. *Acta Psychologica*, 1962, 20, 139–158.

———. Comparing factor trait and state scores across ages and cultures. *J. of Gerontology*, 1969, 24, 348–360.

———. The isopodic and equipotent principles for comparing factor scores across different population. *British J. of Mathematical and Statistical Psychology*, 1970, 23, 23–41.

———. *Abilities: Their Structure, Growth and Action*. Boston: Houghton-Mifflin, 1971.

———. *Real Base, True Zero Factor Analysis*. Multivariate Behavioral Research Monograph, No. 72-1. Fort Worth, Texas: Texas Christian University Press, 1972.

———. Unravelling maturational and learning developments by the comparative MAVA and structured learning approaches. In Nesselroade, J.R., & Reese, J. (Eds.) *Life Span Developmental Psychology*. New York: Academic Press, 1973.

———. *Personality and Mood by Questionnaire*, San Francisco: Jossey Bass, 1973.

———. *The Scientific Use of Factor Analysis in Behavioral and Life Sciences*. New York: Plenum, 1978.

———. *Personality and Learning Theory, Vol. 1*. New York: Springer, 1980.

———. *Personality and Learning Theory, Vol. 2*. New York: Springer, 1981.

———. *The Inheritance of Personality and Ability*. New York: Academic Press, 1982a

———. The psychometry of objective motivation measurement: A response to the critique of Cooper and Kline. *British J. of Educational Psychology*, 1982b, 32, 234–247.

———. The spectrad development of attribution theory into spectrad theory using the general perceptual model. *Multivariate Behavioral Research*, 1982c, 17, 169–192.

Cattell, R.B. & Baggaley, A.R. The objective measurement of attitude motivation measurement development. *J. of Personality*, 1956, 24, 401–423.

Cattell, R.B. & Barton, K. Changes in psychological state measures with time of day. *Psychological Reports*, 1974, 35, 219–222.

Cattell, R.B. & Birkett, H. Can P-technique diagnosis be practicably shortened? Some proposals and test of a 50–day abridgement. *Multivariate Experimental Clinical Research*, 1980, 5, 1–16.

Cattell, R.B. & Birkett, H., The known personality factors found aligned between first order T-data & second order Q -data factors with new evidence on the control, independence, and regression traits. *Personality and Individual Differences*, 1980, 1, 229–238.

Cattell, R.B., Blaine, D.D., & Brennan, J. N-way factor analysis for obtaining personality environment test contributions to any response. A plasmode illustration. In Snyder, H. & Law, B.(Eds.) *N-Mode and N-Way Factoring*. Brisbane, Australia: Queensland University Press, 1984.

Cattell, R.B. & Brennan, J. State measurement: A check on the fit of the modulation theory model to anxiety and depression states. *Psychological Bulletin*.

Cattell, R.B. & Butcher, J. *The Prediction of Achievement and Creativity*. Indianapolis: Bobbs-Merrill, 1968.

Cattell, R.B. & Carter, M. *Development of the superego, G, and its relatives, from age 10 to adulthood*. (in press) 1985.

Cattell, R.B. & Child, D. *Motivation and Dynamic Structure*. New York: Holt, 1975.

Cattell, R.B. & Cross, K.P. Comparison of the ergic and self-sentiment structures found in dynamic traits by R- and P-techniques. *J. of Personality*, 1952, 21, 250–271.

Cattell, R.B., DeYoung, Y.E., & Horn, J.L. Human motives as dynamic states: A dR analysis of objective motivation measures. *Multivariate Experimental Clinical Psychology*, 1974, 1, 58–78.

Cattell, R.B. & Dielman, T.E. The structure of motivation manifestations as measured in the laboratory rat: An examination of motivation component theory. *Social Behavior and Personality*, 1974, 2, 10–24.

Cattell, R.B., Eber, H.J., & Tatsuoka, M. *Handbook for the 16PF Test*. Champaign, Ill.: IPAT, 1970.

Cattell, R.B., Heist, A.B., Heist, O.P., & Stewart, R.G. The objective measurement of dynamic traits. *Educational and Psychological Measurement*, 1950, 10, 229–248.

Cattell, R.B. & Horn, J.L. An integrating study of the factor structure of adult attitude interests. *Genetic Psychology Monographs*, 1963, 67, 89–149.

Cattell, R.B., Horn, J.L., & Butcher, J. The dynamic structures of attitudes in adults. A description of some established factors of their measurement in the Motivation Analysis Test (MAT). *British J. of Psychology*, 1962, 53, 57–69.

Cattell, R.B., Kawash, G.F., & DeYoung, G.E. Validation of objective measures of ergic tension. Response of the sex erg to visual stimulation. *J. of Experimental Research in Personality*, 1972, 6, 76–83.

Cattell, R.B., Lawlis, F., McGill, J., & McGraw, C. A check on the structure & meaning of primary motivation components. *Multivariate Experimental Clinical Research*, 1978, 4, 1–10.

Cattell, R.B. & Luborsky, L.B. P-technique demonstrated as a new clinical method for determining personality and symptom structure. *J. of General Psychology*, 1950, 42, 3–24.

Cattell, R.B., Maxwell, E.F., Light, B.H., & Unger, M.P. The objective measurement of attitudes. *British J. of Psychology*, 1949, 40, 81–90.

Cattell, R.B., McGill, J.C., Lawlis, Y.I., & McGraw, P. Experimental check on the theory of motivational components, duplicated in two interest areas. *Multivariate Experimental Clinical Research*, 1979, 4, 33–52.

Cattell, R.B., Radcliffe, J., & Sweney, A.B. The nature of measurement of components of motivation. *Genetic Psychology Monographs*, 1963, 68, 49–211.

Cattell, R.B., et al. The effects of psychotherapy upon measured anxiety and regression. *American J. of Psychotherapy*, 1966, 20, 261–269.

Cattell, R.B. & Scheier, I.H. *The Meaning and Measurement of Anxiety and Neurosis*. New York: Ronald, 1961.

Cattell, R.B., Schmidt, L.B., & Bjersted, A. Clinical diagnosis by the Objective-Analytic Personality Batteries. *J. of Clinical Psychology Monograph Supplements*, 1972, 34, 1–78.

Cattell, R.B. & Sweney, A.B. Components measurable in manifestations of mental conflict. *J. of Abnormal & Social Psychology*, 1964, 68, 479–490.

Cattell, R.B. & Warburton, F.W. *Objective Personality and Motivation Tests*. Urbana: University of Illinois Press, 1967.

Cattell, R.B. & Wenig, P. Dynamic and cognitive factors controlling misperception. *J. of Abnormal & Social Psychology*, 1952, 47, 797–809.

Child, D. *The Essentials of Factor Analysis*. London: Holt, 1970.

Cooper, C. & Kline, P. The internal structure of the Motivation Analysis Test. *British J. of Educational Psychology*, 1982, 52, 228–233.

Crissy, W.J. & Daniel, W.J. Vocational interest factors in women. *J. of Applied Psychology*, 1939, 23, 488–494.

Curran, J.P. The dimensions of state change in Q-data and chain P-technique, on twenty women. Unpublished M.A. Thesis, University of Illinois, Urbana, 1968.

Curran, J.P. & Cattell, R.B. *The Eight State Battery*, Champaign, Illinois: IPAT, 1976

Das, R.S. An investigation of attitude structure and some hypothesized personality correlates. Unpublished Ph.D. Dissertation, University of Illinois, Urbana, 1955.

Deese, J. & Hulse, S.H. *The Psychology of Learning.* New York: McGraw-Hill, 1967.

Delhees, K.H., Cattell, R.B., & Sweney, A.B. The objective measurement of children's intrafamilial attitude and sentiment structure. *J. Genetic Psychology,* 1971, 188, 87–113.

DeYoung, G.E., Cattell, R.B., Gabonit, M., & Barton, K. A causal model of effects of personality and marital role factors upon diary reported sexual behavior. *Proceedings of the 81st Annual Meeting of the APA,* Montreal, Canada, 1973, 8, 357–358.

Drevdahl, J.E., & Cattell, R.B. Personality and creativity in artists and writers. *J. of Clinical Psychology,* 1958, 14, 107–111.

Duffy, E. *Activation and behavior.* New York: Wiley, 1962.

Egger, M.D. & Miller, N.E. When is reward reinforcing? An experimental study of the information hypothesis. *J. of Comparative and Physiological Psychology,* 1963, 56, 132–137.

Endler, N.S. & Hunt, J. McV. Generalizability of contributions from sources of variance in the S-R inventories of anxiousness. *J. of Personality,* 1969, 37, 1–24.

Estes, W.K. Burke, C.J., Atkinson, R.C., & Frankmann, J.B. Probabalistic discrimination learning. *J. of Experimental Psychology,* 1957, 47, 225–234.

Eysenck, H.J. *Dimensions of Personality.* London: Kagan Paul, 1947.

Eysenck, H.J. *The Biological Bases of Personality.* Springfield, Illinois: Thomas, 1967.

Festinger, L. *A theory of cognitive dissonance.* Stanford: Stanford University Press, 1962.

Fleishman, E.A. Development of a behavior taxonomy for describing human tasks: A correlational experimental approach. *J. of Applied Psychology,* 1967, 51, 1–10.

Forgus, R.H. Early visual and motor experience as determiners of complex maze learning ability. *J. of Comparative and Physiological Psychology,* 1955, 48, 215–220.

Freud, S. *Instincts and their Vicissitudes.* Collected papers. New York: Collier, 1915.

Gorsuch, R.L. *Factor Analysis.* London: Saunders, 1974.

Guilford, J.P., Christenson, P.B., Bond, N.A., & Sutton, M.A. A factor analysis of human interests. *Psychological Monographs,* 1954, 68: 4.

Gundlach, R.H. & Gerum, E. Vocational interests and types of abilities. *J. of Educational Psychology,* 1931, 22, 505-515.

Hall, J.F. & Kubrick, J.L. The relationship between the measures of response strength. *J. of Comparative and Physiological Psychology,* 1952, 45, 280–282.

Hammond, W.H. An analysis of youth center interests. *British J. of Educational Psychology,* 1945, 15, 122–126.

Harlow, H.F. & Harlow, M.K. Social deprivation in monkeys. *Scientific American*, 1962, 207, 137–146.

Harlow, H.F. & Harlow, M.K. The affectional systems. In Schrier, A.M., Harlow, H.F., & Stollnitz, F. (Eds.) *Behavior of Non-human Primates.* New York: Academic Press, 1965.

Hendricks, B.C. The sensitivity of the dynamic calculus to short term changes in interest structure. Unpublished M.A. Thesis, University of Illinois, Urbana, 1971.

Hess, E.H. Imprinting in animals. *Scientific American*, 1958, 198, 81–90.

Horn, J.L. & Sweney, A.B. The dynamic calculus model for motivation and its use in understanding the individual case. In A.B. Mahrer (Ed.) *New Approaches to Personality Classification.* New York: Columbia University Press, 1970.

Horst, P. *Matrix Algebra for Social Scientists.* New York: Holt, 1963.

Hull, C.L. *A Behavior System.* New Haven: Yale University Press, 1952.

Ikin, A.G., Pear, T.H., & Thouless, R.H. The psychogalvanic phenomenon in dream analysis. *British J. of Psychology*, 1924, 5, 23–43.

Inhelder, B. & Piaget, J. *The growth of logical thinking from childhood to adolescence.* New York: Basic Books, 1958.

James, W. *Principles of Psychology*, New York, Holt, 1890.

Kawash, G.W., Dielman, F.E., & Cattell, R.B. Changes in objective measures of fear motivation as a function of laboratory controlled motivation. *Psychological Reports*, 1972, 30, 59–63.

Kline, P. & Grindley, J. A 28–day case study with the MAT. *J. Multivariate Experimental Clinical Psychology*, 1974, 1, 13-22.

Koestler, A. *The Ghost in the Machine.* New York: Macmillan, 1967.

Kohlberg, L. Moralization: the cognitive developmental approach. In Baltes, P. & Schaig, W. (Eds.) *Life span developmental psychology.* New York: Academic Press, 1973.

Konorski, J. *Conditioned Reflexes and Neuron Organization.* New York: Cambridge U niversity Press, 1948.

Korth, B. Attitude Change in relation to reward and initial dynamic structure. Unpublished M.A. Thesis, University of Illinois, Urbana, 1970.

Krug, S.E. An examination of experimentally induced changes in ergic tension levels. Unpublished M.A. thesis, University of Illinois, Urbana, 1969.

Krug, S.E. An examination of experimentally induced changes in ergic tension levels. Unpublished Ph.D. Dissertation, University of Illinois, Urbana, 1971.

Laughlin, J. Prediction of action decisions from the dynamic calculus. Unpublished M.A. thesis, University of Illinois, Urbana, 1973.

Lawlis, G.F. Motivational factors affecting employment stability. *J. of Social Psychology*, 1971, 84, 215–225.

Lorenz, K. *On aggression.* London: Methuen, 1967.

Madsen, K.B. *Theories of Motivation.* Copenhagen: Munksgard, 1968.

Madsen, K.B. *Modern Theories of Motivation.* Copenhagen: Munksgard, 1974.

Magnusson, D. The person and the situation in an interactional model of behavior. *Scandinavian J. of Psychology.* 1976, 17, 253–277.

MacCorquadale, K. & Meehl, P. On the elimination of blind entries without obvious reinforcement. *J. of Comparative and Physiological Psychology,* 1957, 44, 367–371.

McDougall, W. *The Energies of Men.* London: Methuen, 1932.

Mackintosh, N..J. *The Psychology of Animal Learning.* Lonodon: Academic Press, 1974.

Maslow, A.H. Appetites and hungers in animal motivation. *J. of Comparative Psychology,* 1935, 20, 75–83.

Maslow, A.H. *Motivation and Personality.* New York: Harper, 1970.

May, J.M. & Sweney, A.B. Personality and motivation changes observed in the treatment of psychotic patients. *Paper of Southwestern Psychological Association Annual Meeting,* 1965.

Meehl, P.E. & MacCorquadale, K. A further study of latent learning in the T-maze. *J. of Comparative Physiological Psychology,* 1948, 41, 372–396.

Miller, J.G. *Living Systems.* New York: McGraw-Hill, 1970.

Muktananda, B. *Play of Consciousness.* Los Angeles: Ashram, 1974.

Murray, H.A. *Explorations in Personality.* New York: Oxford University Press, 1938.

Pribram, K.H. The new neurology and the biology of emotion. *American Psychologist,* 1967, 22, 830–838.

Rapaport, D. The structure of psychoanalytic theory. *Psychological Issues,* 1960, 2:6.

Renner, K.E. Temporal integration: The relative value, of rewards and punishments as a function of their temporal distance from the response. *J. of Experimental Psychology,* 1966, 71, 902–907.

Rescorla, R.A. & Solomon, R.C. Two process learning theory, relationships between Pavlovian conditioning and instrumental learning. *Psychological Review,* 1967, 94, 151–182.

Royce, J.R. & Buss, A.R. The role of general systems and information theory in multi-factor individuality theory. *Canadian Psychological Review,* 1976, 17, 1–21.

Royce, J.R. & Covington, M. Genetic differences in the avoidance conditioning of mice. *J. of Comparative & Physiological Psychology,* 1960, 53, 197–200.

Scriven, M. The mechanical concept of mind. In Sayne, K.M. (Ed.) *The Modelling of Mind.* New York: University of Notre Dame, 1963.

Shearer, D. The direction of memory by emotional, ergic states. Ph.D. Dissertation, Hawaii School of Professional Psychology, Honolulu, 1984.

Sheffield, F.D., Wulff, J.J., & Backer, R. Reward value of copulation without sex drive reduction. *J. of Comparative and Physiological Psychology*, 1951, 44, 3–8.

Shotwell, A., Hurley, J., & Cattell, R.B. Motivational structure of a hospitalized mental defective. *J. of Abnormal and Social Psychology*, 1961, 62, 423–426.

Smuts, J. *Holism and Evolution*. New York: Macmillan, 1926.

Spearman, C. *The Nature of Intelligence and the Principles of Cognition*. London: Macmillan, 1923.

Spence, K.W. & Taylor, J. Anxiety and the strength of the UCS as determiners of the amount of eyelid conditioning. *J. of Experimental Psychology*, 1951, 42, 183–188.

Spielberger, C.D. *Anxiety: Current Trends in Theory and Research*. New York: Academic Press, 1973.

Strong, E.K. *Vocational Interests of Men and Women*. Stanford: Stanford University Press, 1949.

Sweney, A.B. Objective measurement of strength of dynamic structure factors, pp. 148–186. In Cattell, R.B. & Warburton, F.W. (Eds.) *Objective Personality and Motivation Tests*. Urbana, Illinois: University of Illinois Press, 1967.

Sweney, A.B. & Cattell, R.B. Dynamic factors in 12-year old children as revealed in measures of integrated motivation. *J. Clinical Psychology*, 1961, 17, 366–369.

Thorndike, E.L. The interests of adults. 2. The interrelations of adult interest. *J. of Educational Psychology*, 1935, 26, 497–507.

Thurstone, L.L. A multiple factor study of vocational interests. *J. of Personality*, 1935, 10, 198–205.

Tinbergen, N. *A Study of Instinct*. Oxford: Oxford University Press, 1951.

Torr, D.V. A factor analysis of 49 interest variables. Annual Research Bulletin, 1953, Human Resources Research Center, ARDC Lachland Air Force Base, Texas.

Vaughan, D.S. A test of Cattell's structured learning theory. Unpublished M.A. Thesis, University of Illinois, Urbana, 1973.

Vernon, P.E. Classifying high grade occupational interests. *J. of Abnormal and Social Psychology*, 1949, 44, 85–96..

Wessman, A.E. & Ricks, D.F. *Mood and Personality*. New York: Holt, 1966.

Williams, J.R. A test of the validity of P-technique in the measurement of internal conflict. *J. of Personality*, 1959, 27, 418–437.

Woliver, R.E. & Cattell, R.B. Data on the "equity" theory of marriage by objective dynamic measures. *International J. of Psychology*, 1981, 16, 170–198.

Young, P.T. *Motivation and Emotion*. New York: Wiley, 1961.

Subject Index

Name Index

About the Author

Professor Raymond B. Cattell has taught personality and social psychology at Clark, Duke, Harvard, Hawaii, Illinois and London (Exeter) Universities. From 1945 to 1973 he directed the Laboratory of Personality and Group Behavior Research, as Distinguished Research Professor, at the University of Illinois, with a group of research associates from several countries, now famous in their own fields.

He has received the Darwin Fellowship, the Wenner Gren prize of the New York Academy of Science, the citation for contribution to psychometrics from ETS and APA, and the first presidency of the Society of Multivariate Experimental Psychology, among other distinctions. His over 50 years of contributions has covered personality and ability structure, group behavior, national culture patterns, genetics, the dynamic calculus, numerous contributions to experimental statistical methods, and the system of structured learning theory. The present book puts in a nutshell the whole development of dynamic theory and the dynamic calculus.

Due